MILAN
ENCOUNTER

DONNA WHEELER

Milan Encounter

Published by Lonely Planet Publications Pty Ltd
ABN 36 005 607 983

Australia	Head Office, Locked Bag 1, Footscray, Victoria 3011 ☎ 03 8379 8000 fax 03 8379 8111 talk2us@lonelyplanet.com.au
USA	150 Linden St, Oakland, CA 94607 ☎ 510 250 6400 toll free 800 275 8555 fax 510 893 8572 info@lonelyplanet.com
UK	2nd fl, 186 City Rd, London EC1V 2NT ☎ 020 7106 2100 fax 020 7106 2101 go@lonelyplanet.co.uk

This title was commissioned in Lonely Planet's London office and produced by: **Commissioning Editor** Paula Hardy **Coordinating Editor** Justin Flynn **Coordinating Cartographer** James Regan **Layout Designers** Indra Kilfoyle, Katherine Marsh **Assisting Editors** Victoria Harrison, Simone Egger, Erin Richards **Assisting Cartographer** Fatima Basic **Managing Editor** Sasha Baskett **Managing Cartographer** Mark Griffiths **Managing Layout Designers** Laura Jane, Celia Wood **Cover Designer** Tamsin Wilson **Project Manager** Ruth Cosgrove **Series Designer** Mik Ruff **Language Content Coordinator** Quentin Frayne **Thanks to** Shahara Ahmed, Jennifer Garrett, Lisa Knights, Trent Paton, Lyahna Spencer

ISBN 978 1 74104 994 7

Printed by Hang Tai Printing Company.
Printed in China.

HOW TO USE THIS BOOK
Colour-Coding & Maps
Colour-coding is used for symbols on maps and in the text that they relate to (eg all eating venues on the maps and in the text are given a green knife and fork symbol). Each neighbourhood also gets its own colour, and this is used down the edge of the page and throughout that neighbourhood section.

Shaded yellow areas on the maps denote 'areas of interest' – for their historical significance, their attractive architecture or their great bars and restaurants. We encourage you to head to these areas and just start exploring!

Prices
Multiple prices listed with reviews (eg €10/5 or €10/5/20) indicate adult/child, adult/concession or adult/child/family.

Send us your feedback We love to hear from readers – your comments help make our books better. We read every word you send us, and we always guarantee that your feedback goes straight to the appropriate authors. The most useful submissions are rewarded with a free book. To send us your updates and find out about Lonely Planet events, newsletters and travel news visit our award-winning website: *lonelyplanet.com/contact*

Note: We may edit, reproduce and incorporate your comments in Lonely Planet products such as guidebooks, websites and digital products, so let us know if you don't want your comments reproduced or your name acknowledged. For a copy of our privacy policy visit *lonelyplanet.com/privacy*.

DONNA WHEELER

Donna's first impression of Milan was all late-night chaos and models behaving badly. These days it's the city's intriguing architecture, iconic designers, dynamic art scene and penchant for raw fish that lure her back during visits to her husband's family in nearby Piedmonte and Liguria. Not to mention a recurring dream involving Costume National shoes. Donna commissioned restaurant guides and online features inhouse for Lonely Planet. Her careers include editing, digital producing, content strategy and art direction. She has studied visual arts, literature and postgraduate professional writing and editing, and writes on history, art and food. This is her third book for Lonely Planet.

DONNA'S THANKS

Cheers to Lonely Planet's Paula Hardy for precision briefing and patience. Many thanks to Mariangela Marinoni, Gaia Polloni, Gio Terzi and Rico Guarnieri for excellent leads, to Chiara Agnello and Roberta Tenconi for invaluable insights and generosity, and to the travellers from Macclesfield and Liverpool for sharing your experiences. *Mille grazie per la famiglia* Marolo: Eugenio, Pina, Gabri and Matti. To Rebecca Brandon, thank you darling for being part of my life from St Leonards to San Babila. Lastly, much love and thanks to Joe Guario and my sweet girls Rumer and Biba at home in Melbourne.

THE PHOTOGRAPHER

Born in Rome, Paolo Cordelli has been taking pictures since 1991. He works as freelance photographer and also gives lessons in photography, specialising in travel and landscapes. During his career, Paolo has taken photographs in the USA, India, Thailand, Morocco, Tunisia and Italy and many other European countries.

Cover photograph Shu bar, Adam Eastland /Alamy. **Internal photographs** p80, p93, p107, p125, p133 by Donna Wheeler; p27 Jean Schweitzer/Alamy; p21 The Bridgeman Art Library; p47 Giuseppe Cacace/AFP/Getty Images; p172 Giuseppe Cacace/Stringer/Getty Images; p22, p113, p169 Giorgio Majno/FAI - Fondo Ambiente Italiano. All other photographs by Lonely Planet Images, and by Paolo Cordelli except p102 Jon Davison; p4, p6, p8, p11, p13, p19, p26, p29, p31, p34 (bottom left), p34 (bottom right), p36, p38, p62, p64, p142, p173 Martin Moos; p43 Russell Mountford; p23 Dallas Stribley. All images are copyright of the photographers unless otherwise indicated. Many of the images in this guide are available for licensing from **Lonely Planet Images**: www.lonelyplanetimages.com.

Feeding the hungry masses at Piazza del Duomo (p43)

CONTENTS

THE AUTHOR	03	>APERITIVO	162
THIS IS MILAN	07	>FOOD	164
HIGHLIGHTS	08	>DESIGN	166
MILAN DIARY	27	>MUSEUMS &	
ITINERARIES	33	GALLERIES	168
NEIGHBOURHOODS	38	>ARCHITECTURE	169
>AROUND DUOMO	42	>CLUBBING	170
>QUADRILATERO D'ORO		>MUSIC	171
& GIARDINI PUBBLICI	58	>FIERA	172
>BRERA	76	**BACKGROUND**	**174**
>PARCO SEMPIONE	88	**DIRECTORY**	**181**
>CORSO COMO, PORTA		**INDEX**	**193**
GARIBALDI & ISOLA	100		
>SAN BABILA	110		
>PORTA ROMANA &			
THE SOUTH	120		
>NAVIGLI,			
PORTA TICINESE &			
ZONA TORTONA	128		
>CORSO MAGENTA,			
SANT'AMBROGIO &			
THE WEST	140		
EXCURSIONS	**151**		
>BERGAMO	152		
>BELLAGIO	153		
>VERONA	154		
>LAGO MAGGIORE	155		
SNAPSHOTS	**156**		
>ACCOMMODATION	158		
>SHOPPING	160		

THIS IS MILAN

Milan is Italy's city of the future, a fast-paced metropolis where creativity is big business, looking good is compulsory and after-work drinks, *aperitivi*, are an artform.

It's also a city with ancient roots and extraordinary treasures, that, unlike the rest of Italy, you'll quite often get to experience without queues of tourists, touts or a raft of expectations. Flat, featureless and with a grab bag of architectural styles, Milan is often called ugly. We'd rather say it has character. A warren of cobbled streets fans out from the Duomo while historic neighbourhoods like Brera and Navigli have charm worthy of any tourist brochure. Others are lined with stately 19th-century and Liberty apartment buildings and dotted with stunning modernist icons.

'You hear people ask for a 'cappuccio' as if the cappuccino was a diminutive form - the client wants to make sure he isn't being slighted,' novelist Luciano Bianciardi remarked of the Milanese in 1966. Nothing has changed. Milan may look like an introverted, moody town but its 1.3 million inhabitants are indefatigably optimistic, fabulously ambitious, alarmingly stylish and often full of hot, if well-articulated, air. The Milanese, also known as Meneghini or Ambrosiani, aren't as homogeneous as their designer suits and flawless grooming make out. Two economic booms at the start and middle of the 20th century brought generations of immigrants from the south and were joined by Chinese, African, Latin American, indian, Eastern European and Middle Eastern communities.

Milanese don't have time to play nice for visitors, but they're happy to share their own intoxicating round of pursuits, be that precision shopping, following AC or Inter fanatically, browsing edgy contemporary galleries and the world's chicest design showrooms, discovering Italy's most innovative and diverse culinary landscape, listening to live acts from verdito vampire Weekend, clubbing 'til dawn and, of course, loading up a plate with local delicacies while downing an expertly mixed evening Negroni.

Top So much more than a shopping arcade – Galleria Vittorio Emanuele II (p43) **Bottom** The wood-panelled pasticceria, of Marchesi (p53)

>HIGHLIGHTS

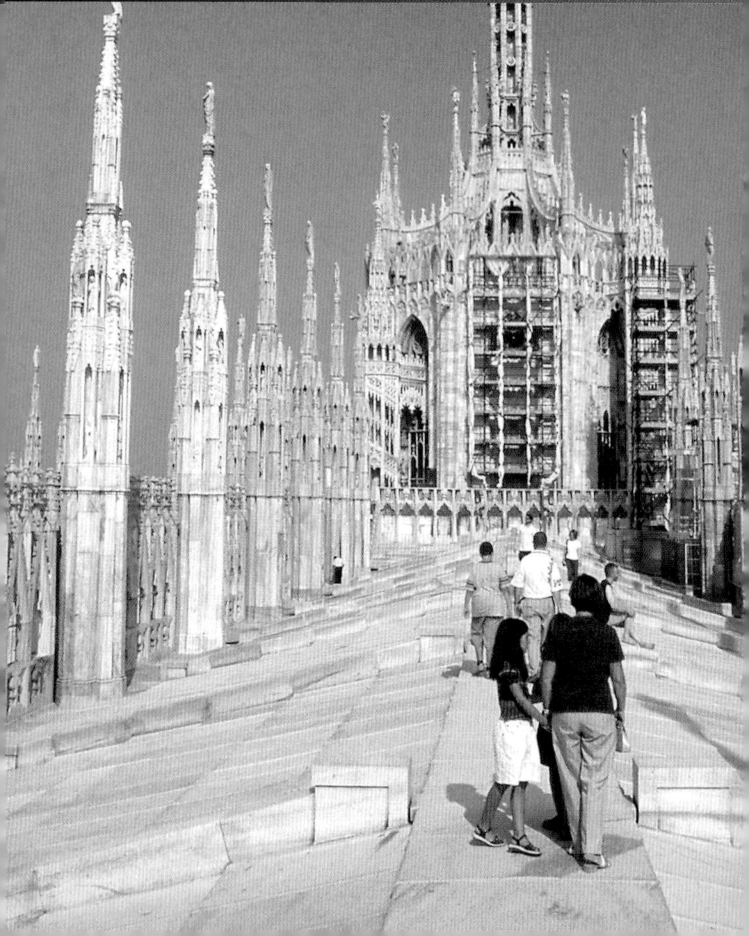

>1 Strut your stuff on Planet Fashion's finest block 10
>2 Gaze up at marble spires or down upon the city 12
>3 Stroll through a grand shopping arcade 14
>4 Sip and graze in the city's famous bars 15
>5 Lose an afternoon in a palazzo of Renaissance
treasures 16
>6 Make like a diva and swoon in the stalls 18
>7 Navigate Navigli's canalside bars and
restaurants 19
>8 Eat up the region's best produce 20
>9 Ponder the power of Leonardo's *Last Supper* 21
>10 Waltz about a magnificent Modernist villa 22
>11 Browse the bounty of Milan's best
antique dealers 23
>12 Connect with Milan's cutting-edge creatives 24
>13 Dream designer dreams in designer sheets 25
>14 Shout GOOOOOOOAAAAAL at San Siro 26

Don't miss the grandeur of Il Duomo (p43)

>1 QUADRILATERO D'ORO

STRUT YOUR STUFF ON PLANET FASHION'S FINEST BLOCK

For anyone interested in the fall of a frock or the cut of a jacket, a stroll around Quadrilatero D'Oro, the world's most famed and fabled shopping district, is on one's lifetime to-do list. This quaintly cobbled quadrangle of streets may have always been synonymous with elegance and money (Via Monte Napoleone was once, fittingly, where Napoleon's government managed loans), but the Quad's legendary fashion status belongs firmly to Milan's postwar reinvention. During the boom years of the 1950s the city's fashion houses established ateliers in the area bounded by Vie Monte Napoleone, Della Spiga, Sant'Andrea and Manozoni. Their customers were soon to follow, though it wasn't until the heady excessive '80s that 'Monte Napo' became known worldwide.

The Quad is booming again, and as the rapacious global marques like Dolce & Gabbana, Armani and Prada gobble up street frontage, the gilding drips down to Via Verri and Corso Venezia. In fact, these days, the big labels don't appear to have boundaries of any sort. The D&G boys will snip your hair and plonk a cocktail in your hand as well as dress you from the knickers up. Roberto Cavalli and Giorgio Armani also go way beyond wardrobe with cafes, restaurants, clubs and homewares while Gianfranco Ferre offers to purify, re-energise and rebalance at their spa.

Among these giants, remnants of the area's traditional, discreet past persist (though don't for a minute think that means their wears are less expensive). You'll find elegant lingerie and layettes at Ars Rosa, sensible outdoor and sportswear at Aspesi, seasonally designed baby carriages at Aprica, handcrafted brushes at G, Lorenzi and serious rocks a plenty at the family-run jewellery ateliers. Newcomer Tom Ford has a foot in both worlds, his three-story villa evoking a clubby men's emporium ready for a visit from 007, while its sharp conceptualisation definitely screams 'now'.

Even if you don't have the slightest urge to sling a swag of glossy carriers over your arm, the people-watching is priceless. Bespoke-suited silver foxes prowl, gazelle-limbed models lope up and down,

perfecting a look of glazed detachment for the coming catwalk shows, and aggressively accessorised matrons crowd the bar at Cova for short blacks, *tramezzini* (sandwiches) and some obligatory flirting with the barristas.

>2 DUOMO

GAZE UP AT MARBLE SPIRES OR DOWN UPON THE CITY

Whether it's your virgin visit to Milan or your 50th, your first glimpse of the city's cathedral can never fail to elicit a gasp of awe. Its cloudy Candoglian marble facade and sky-piercing spires appear out of the chaotic grey maze of streets, a sudden, otherworldly vision.

The Duomo may be the enduring symbol of Milan, but it's a cathedral with a chequered past. Begun by Gian Galeazzo Visconti in 1387, its ambitious design was considered impossible to build. Canals were constructed to transport marble to the centre of town, new technologies were invented to adapt to the never-before-attempted scale. There was also the matter of style. Its Gothic lines went rapidly out of fashion (it was even criticised as being 'too French'), and it took on several different looks as the years, then centuries, dragged on. The Duomo's slow construction made its name a byword for an impossible task (*fabrica del Dom* in the Milanese dialect).

During his stint as King of Italy, Napoleon, never to miss a chance to be associated with something so monumental, offered to fund its completion in 1805. The appointed architect piled on the neo-Gothic details – an homage to the original design that displayed a prescient use of fashion logic, ie everything old is new again. The organic ferment of petrified pinnacles, cusps, buttresses, rampant arches, cyma and acroteria are almost all products of the 19th century. The last gate was completed in the 1960s; shortly after, restoration works began. The Duomo's most recent coat of scaffolding came off in 2008.

Initially designed so Milan's then-population of around 40,000 could fit within, the cathedral's elegant, hysterical and sublimely spiritual architecture can even transport 21st-century types back to a medieval mindset. Inside, once your eyes adjust to the subdued light and surreal proportions (there are five grandiose naves), how but not to stare up, and up, to the largest stained-glass windows in all of Christendom?

Under the ever-watchful gaze of the golden Madonnina, you can also wander between the spires on the roof, feeling just a little closer to heaven. It's said that you can see the Matterhorn on a clear day, but given Milan's notorious haze, you'll probably have to ask in favours from Our Lady to guarantee that.

>3 GALLERIA VITTORIO EMANUELE II

STROLL THROUGH A GRAND SHOPPING ARCADE

Directly across from the Duomo sits Milan's other precocious feat
of engineering. This soaring iron-and-glass neoclassical arcade links
Milan's cathedral to its opera house, La Scala, and heralds the new
industrial Italy of the Risorgimento. Despite churchlike proportions and
a cruciform plan, the Galleria celebrates the gleefully secular: shopping.
Highly innovative for its time, the building has spawned countless
imitators, right down to the glazed-roofed megamalls of today.

Architect Giuseppe Mengoni plummeted to his death on the job
in 1877, just before the 14-year project was complete. To avoid such
bad luck, observe Milanese tradition: head under the vast glass dome
to the mosaic of the bull, and grind your heel firmly into its testicles.
Despite the mascot's daily humiliations, the Taurean spirit of luxury
and gracious sloth still dominate. Prada and Gucci and clamouring
chains mix with the glove shops and milliners of old, and cafes dole
out coffee and Campari to be sipped seated on century-old mosaics.

>4 APERITIVI

SIP AND GRAZE IN THE CITY'S FAMOUS BARS

Milan may not have invented the tradition of taking an *aperitivo* – a predinner drink with snacks on the house – but the Milanese have turned it into an art form. Bars all over town bring on the laden platters from 6pm. To partake, order a Negroni (a potent, slightly medicinal-tasting blend of Campari, Antico Rosso and gin), its spritzy little sister the *sbagliato* which substitutes *prosecco* (sparkling white wine) for the gin, and then fight your way back to the bar or dedicated buffet table.

Offerings can be simple and traditional – house-made *patatine fritte* (crisps), olives and roast almonds – but have become increasingly lavish as bars compete in a city of critical and wandering tastebuds. *Crostini* (little toasts with various savoury toppings), salads, prosciutto, smoked salmon and trays of hot pasta often make dinner unnecessary. Happy hour, Italian-style, doesn't involve enthusiastic swilling; the Milanese can nurse their cocktails through several foraging forays. It's first and foremost about relaxing, catching up, checking each other out and passing judgement on the bar's buffet. Drinking comes a very distant second. See p162 for where to find the city's best.

HIGHLIGHTS

>5 PINACOTECA DI BRERA

LOSE AN AFTERNOON IN A
PALAZZO OF RENAISSANCE TREASURES

Founded in the late 18th century, upstairs from the centuries-old Brera Academy (still one of Italy's most prestigious art schools), the Pinacoteca housed the teaching aids of the day: marble and oils. Napoleon soon added to the collection with priceless works 'borrowed' from various religious orders. The roll call of masters may include a Rembrandt, but you're here to ogle the Italians: Titian, Tintoretto and Veronese, a Caravaggio and the Bellini brothers for starters.

Much of the work has tremendous emotional clout. A Bellini Madonna, clad in a deep, meditative navy blue, is sad-eyed and

resolute; Mantegna's *Lamentation over the Dead Christ* is brutal and unsentimental in its violent foreshortening of Christ's corpse; *Christ Scorned* by Bazzi, better known as 'il Sodomo', uses every Mannerist trick in the book to reveal the tragic heart of the Jesus narrative. Biblical set-pieces appear over and over and reveal, through their differences, as much about the temper of their times as they do about the sacred.

The number of pious treasures is exhausting. Take a break and see conservators at work in a climate-controlled glass box, visit the small but luminous collection of Italian Modernists, including the spirituality of Morandi, or join dread-locked art students downstairs for a post life-drawing class Peroni.

>6 A NIGHT AT LA SCALA

MAKE LIKE A DIVA AND SWOON IN THE STALLS

Stendhal had an attack of his very own syndrome on meeting Byron in a Marquis' box at La Scala in 1816, and he certainly wasn't the last person to come over a little faint in the world's most legendary concert hall. A recent renovation took place mostly behind the scenes (superior acoustics and bilingual libretto screens on the back of seats are some of its public face); the charm remains resolutely of the 18th century.

Six stories of *loggia* (boxes and galleries) are bedecked in gilt and lined in crimson, and, for evening performances at least, audiences are similarly turned out. Milanese money, old and new, is deliciously on display. Let the theatrics continue at interval in La Scala's lovely jewel box of a bar or nearby Il Marchesi, with a glass of sparkling and a game of spot the mistress. 'Opera remains the most boring thing in the world,' siged Stendhal, 'if it doesn't succeed in making us daydream about the secret sorrows that disturb the most apparently happy lives'. La Scala: the perfect place to let the reverie take hold.

>7 NAVIGLI

NAVIGATE NAVIGLI'S CANALSIDE BARS AND RESTAURANTS

The Navigli neighbourhood is named after its most identifiable feature – canals – and was, until mid-last-century, a working class area of ancient docks, laundries and warehouses. The Navigli Grande grew from an irrigation ditch to one of the city's busiest thoroughfares in the 1200s. Canals were the autostrade of medieval Milan, and got salt, oil, cheese and wine to town in a timely fashion. More canals were built to deliver marble for constructing the Duomo; filled and paved, many of these now serve as Milan's ring-roads.

After a brief desolate spell when the docks closed in the 1960s and '70s, Navigli's tangle of streets, turbid waterways and pretty iron bridges drew Milan's savvy artists and musicians. It soon usurped Brera as the city's Bohemian 'burb. It may now have well and truly lost its subversive edge, but it's managed to resist the glib glossification of other Milanese neighbourhoods. And the city's most scenic restaurants, liveliest bars, and innovative, individual shops are still here.

>8 DELI DELICIOUS

EAT UP THE REGION'S BEST PRODUCE

Milan's shopping ops don't stop at clothes, accessories, design pieces and antiques. There's a wealth of specialist food emporiums catering for the casually greedy and the full-blown connoisseur.

The centre of town boasts two gourmet meccas, the veritable Peck and Rinascente's new 7th-floor Food Hall. Both offer an impressive range of goods: Italian staples like pasta, oils, preserves, biscotti and wine, as well as cheeses, meats, pastries and chocolates. They both also have on-site cafes and restaurants to appease browsing-induced hunger. Turin's Slow Food venture, Eataly, where everything is sourced from small-scale artisan producers, has also recently set up shop.

Smaller specialist shops dot the city: *alimentari* and *salumaria* (delicatessens) dishing up both Lombard and regional delicacies; *enoteca* (wine shops); chocolate shops; *pasticceria*, which as well as selling signature *pannetone*, pastries and biscuits, also often make their own quaintly traditional chocolates and confectionery. Milan's markets shouldn't be overlooked either, with the region's best produce often to be snapped up for a song.

>9 IL CENACOLO

PONDER THE POWER OF LEONARDO'S LAST SUPPER

When Leonardo da Vinci was at work on the *La Cenacolo* (Last Supper) a star-struck monk noted that he would sometimes arrive in the morning, stare at yesterday's effort, then promptly call it quits for the day. Your visit too will be a similarly brief, intense 15 minutes of ponder before you're deposited back onto Corso Magenta. The clock may be ticking (and it's no mean feat nabbing a ticket in the first place) but the baggage of a thousand dodgy reproductions and one very dubious best-selling novel are quickly shed once actually face to face with the work itself.

Da Vinci's extreme experimental techniques and years of abuse have left the painting faded and perilously fragile, despite 20 years of sophisticated, though often controversial, preservation efforts. But its condition does nothing to lessen the astonishing beauty and enthralling psychological drama before you. Stare at the ethereal, lucent windows beyond the narrative action and you'll wonder if da Vinci's uncharacteristic short-sightedness wasn't divinely inspired.

>10 VILLA NECCHI-CAMPIGLIO

WALTZ ABOUT A MAGNIFICENT MODERNIST VILLA

No matter how concerted your peeking, towering gates, grand wooden doors and eagle-eyed concierges shield the homes of Milan's haute-bourgeoisie. But since its 2008 reopening, you're welcome to wander up the winding garden path to Villa Necchi-Campiglio.

This exquisitely restored 1930s villa was designed by Rationalist architect Piero Portaluppi for Pavian heiresses Nedda and Gigina Necchi, and Gigina's husband Angelo Campiglio. The trio were proud owners of one of the only private swimming pools in Milan, as well as terrarium-faced sunrooms and streamlined electronic shuttering.

Portaluppi's commingling of Art Deco and Rationalist styles powerfully evokes a cusp; the house symbolises an outlook that was astoundingly modern while at the same time desperately anchored in a world that was fast slipping away. Quotidian details – Bauhaus-influenced monograms born on hair brushes and bone china, luggage ready for the sisters' many overseas jaunts, a kitchen cupboard full of pressed linen, silk evening frocks hanging at the ready – are as equally enthralling as the sleek architectural lines and big ticket artworks by Morandi and de Chirico.

>11 MERCATORE ANTIQUARIO DI NAVIGLI

BROWSE THE BOUNTY OF MILAN'S BEST ANTIQUE DEALERS

Come the last Sunday of every month over 400 well-vetted antique and secondhand traders set up along a 2km stretch of the Navigli Grande. There's a fascinating mix of high-quality antiques, including paintings, glass art and antiquities. You'll find yourself dreaming of that 2nd-century Syrian ring for years to come if you (or your credit card) decline. Smaller budgets or suitcase space are well catered for by wonderful flea-market staples: mint-condition '70s sunglasses, mid-century ceramics and antique monogrammed linen. Or detour to Via Corsico for vintage clothes. Although the ambience is casual, bargains are rare; prices tend to be fair but not that far below retail. Milanese buyers and sellers both know their stuff. Local bars and *osterie* (restaurants) are happy to refuel hungry browsers or pop the Prosecco to help celebrate purchases.

>12 CONTEMPORARY ART

CONNECT WITH MILAN'S CUTTING-EDGE CREATIVES

Milan's creative reputation is usually linked to the fashion and design industry, but the city's contemporary art scene is, with neighbouring Turin, the most dynamic in Italy. The majority of Italy's living artists choose to call Milan home, at least between sojourns in New York or Berlin, and there's a network of commercial galleries gathered under the **StartMilano** (www.start-mi.net) umbrella. Most galleries once clustered in Brera, near the city's famous art school, though they are now spread around the city. Lambrate's Via Ventura is emerging as a mini-Chelsea, with a handful of excellent galleries, including seminal Galleria Massimo De Carlo (p104), the bookshop Art Book Milano (p104), and a Saturday afternoon tradition of gallery-hopping.

Although there is currently no large-scale public museum of contemporary art, the void is filled by dynamic private *fondazioni* (foundations). Prada, Trussardi, Hangar Bicocca and Pomodoro all stage programmes of important, ground-breaking work. These shows are well worth looking out for; they're attention grabbing in scale and often competitive in the provocation stakes.

>13 LIVING BY DESIGN

DREAM DESIGNER DREAMS IN DESIGNER SHEETS

Milan's furniture fair and fashion weeks see the design industry cosy up and do business, but in this design-driven town, it's not just a coterie of insiders who get to have all the oh-so-considered fun. Replacing old-world pomp with contemporary brio is a new clutch of design hotels, ready to immerse guests in the city's signature high style. These include the Bulgari Hotel, '7 star' Town House Galleria, Zona Tortona's Nhow, art-clad Spadari and organic-minimal Straff. They're joined by superstylish B&Bs: Carla Sozzani's vintage-luxe 3Rooms at 10 Corso Como or design classic-strewn Foresteria Monforte. Milanese fashion houses have branched out into spas, bars and restaurants too. Wiggle it at Armani Prive, people-watch at Just Cavalli, do *aperitivo* at Patrizia Pepe's Living or have it shaken or stirred at Dolce & Gabbana's Martini Bar. Crass commercialism or clever brand stratification? To the Milanese it's just a natural extension of *la vita moda*.

>14 FOOTBALL
SHOUT GOOOOOOOAAAAAL AT SAN SIRO

Unlike the Duomo, San Siro Stadium wasn't designed to hold the entire population of Milan but on a Sunday afternoon amid 85,000 football-mad citizens, it can certainly feel like it. The city's two clubs, AC Milan and FC Internazionale Milano (aka Inter), play on alternate weeks. *Tiforsi* (rabid fans) band together as *ultras* (cheer squads), cluster at the *curva nord* (north curve) or *curva sud* (south curve) of the stadium. Chants bellowed from the *curvas* might include standard stadium anthems 'Guantanamera', 'Seven Nation Army' or 'You'll Never Walk Alone', but also 'Bella, Ciao!', a cracking WWII partisan song, and 'O Mia Bela Mudunina', a semi-ironic paean to the city's golden mascot, the Madonnina. Violence is rare, though not unheard of, but the *tiforsi* are highly territorial and generally keep to themselves. And the 20-minute walk of shame or triumph back to the Lotto metro stop can be almost as colourful as the match itself.

>MILAN DIARY

Milan might present a serious, industrious face to the world, but that doesn't mean it doesn't know how to get festive. In fact, the Milanese have a knack for turning business into a city-wide party – just look at Fashion Week and the Salone del Mobile. The city hosts an enormous array of cultural and sporting events year round. Even Milan's steamy summer, usually the time Milanese get out of town, boasts an increasing number of music, art and street festivals. Events listings can be found in the Corriere della Sera's Vivimilano (www.vivimilano.it, in Italian), Zero (milano.zero .eu, in Italian) and the English-language Hello Milano (www.hellomilano.it).

Football fans congregate around Il Duomo (p43)

JANUARY

Corteo dei Re Magi

The original three wise guys hit town for this parade from the Piazza Duomo to the Church of Sant'Eustorgio to celebrate Epiphany on 6 January.

Winter Sales

Sales begin at all shops on the same day, so check the local press for the official date as well as details of special late-night shopping openings.

FEBRUARY

Carnevale Ambrosian

Lent comes late to the Milanese Ambrosian church, with Carnevale sensibly held on the Saturday that falls after everyone else's frantic Fat Tuesday. Traditionally costumed revellers – think striped hose and silly hats in lieu of sparkly thongs and headdresses – take to the streets and the Piazza del Duomo.

Capodanno Cinese

Milan's Chinatown in Via Paolo Sarpi hosts a large Chinese New Year parade with traditional drummers, dragons, fireworks and the occasional Italian touch; a *bersaglieri fanfara* (Piedmontese brass army band) have been known to join in.

APRIL

Lunedì dell'Angelo

This Franciscan flower market marks the beginning of spring. Stalls take over Piazza Sant'Angelo and the streets between Piazza di Repubblica and Brera. It has been held on Pasquetta – Easter Monday – for more than 400 years. Handicrafts, books and food are also sold.

MiArt

www.miart.it

Milan's annual modern and contemporary art fair may not be Basel but it attracts more than 30,000 art lovers, more than

CATWALK CALL SHEET

Glimpse the future of wardrobes worldwide four times a year, when designers parade next season's collections at the seasonal Milan Fashion Weeks.

The men's shows head the A/W (autumn/winter) schedule in January, with the women's following in February. Men's S/S (spring/summer) take place in June and the women's in September. For event listings and a full timetable of designer showcases, check with the Camera Nazionale della Moda Italiana (National Chamber of Italian Fashion; www.camera moda.it/eng).

If you can't snare a pass, *UK Vogue* (www.vogue.co.uk) has up-to-the-minute photographic coverage, useful for being in the know during the *aperitivo*-hour post-show analysis.

MILAN DIARY

200 exhibitors and increasing amounts of international attention. It's held at fieramilanocity.

Salone Internazionale del Mobile

www.cosmit.it

Designers, architects and decor junkies descend upon Milan to check out chairs, colour swatches and the way we live now. The world's most prestigious (and profit-driven) furniture fair is held annually at fieramilano (Rho), with satellite exhibitions in Zona Tortona. The main fair is joined in alternate years by lighting, accessories, office, kitchen and bathroom shows too.

MAY

Cortili Aperti

www.italiamultimedia.com/cortiliaperti/

For one May Sunday, the gates to some of the city's most beautiful private courtyards are flung open, no invitation or plaintive pleading required. Print out a map and make your own itinerary.

JUNE

Christopher Street Day

www.pridemilano.org

Milan's Pride March is held in mid-June with the rainbow flag waved from Via Palestro, through the Piazza Duomo to an after-party at Piazza Castello.

Winter and summer sales are a shopper's delight

Festa del Naviglio

Music, food, parades and special events in the city's canal district.

Giro d'Italia

www.ilgiroditalia.it

Cheer on the pink at the finish line as this gruelling three-week world-famous cycling race winds up.

International Gay & Lesbian Milan Film Festival

www.cinemagaylesbico.com

Week-long cinematic celebration of gay/lesbian/bi/trans life at the Teatro Strehler.

La Bella Estate

www.comune.milano.it

More than 400 concerts, exhibitions and family events are organised by the city government to entertain those who haven't escaped to the lakes or beach during June, July and August.

Monlue Festival

www.estateamonlue.it

World, folk and reggae concerts are held at this country estate near Linate airport.

JULY

Latin American Festival

www.latinoamericando.it

Milan's large Latin-American community gets the city dancing to the beat in a three-month series of concerts as well as celebrating the region's architecture, literature and food.

Milano Jazzin Festival

www.milanojazzinfestival.com

Let them call it jazz, though the international line up that plays Arena Civica actually includes everything from indie to pop giants and, yes, the odd old horn player.

Villa Arconati Festival

www.insiemegroane.it/festivalarconati/

The baroque garden of this *Villa di Delizia* on the outskirts of Milan plays host to a variety of international talent – from Cesaria Evora

to Patti Smith to Erykah Badu – in a series of balmy night concerts.

Summer Sales

Sales begin at all shops on the same day, so check the local press for the official date as well as details of special late-night shopping openings.

SEPTEMBER

Football Season

www.sansiro.net

Life begins again for football fans, be they AC Milan or Inter, when the Serie A season kicks off at San Siro Stadium.

Italian F1 Grand Prix

www.monzanet.it

Monza's historic autodrome hosts the F1 circuit 20km north of Milan.

Milano Film Festival

www.milanofilmfestival.it/eng/

Ten days of international features, shorts and retrospectives at the Teatro Piccolo as well as open-air screenings, music and parties at Parco Sempione.

Milano Musica Festival

www.milanomusica.org

This international festival highlights contemporary composition in a month-long series of concerts and conferences held throughout the city and at La Scala.

Music festivals and concerts are an important part of Milan's vibrant street scene

La Nivola e il Santo Chiodo

See the Archbishop of Milan ascend to the Duomo's chancel roof in a cloud-adorned basket; he's up there to retrieve what is supposedly one of the nails from Christ's cross (fashioned, bizarrely, by Constantine into a horse's bridle).

OCTOBER

Vinilmania

www.vinilmaniaitalia.com

Held at the Parco Esposizioni Novegro, this record fair draws the vinyl cultists as well as casual CD collectors. There are also fairs in May and February.

NOVEMBER

Milan City Marathon

milanocitymarathon.gazzetta.it

Join 5000 runners on this super flat, super fast marathon that starts and finishes at the Castello Sforzesco.

DECEMBER

Festa di Sant'Ambrogio & Fiera degli Obei Obei

The feast day of Milan's patron saint is celebrated on 7 December with a large Christmas fair. It goes by the name Obej! Obej! (pronounced o-bay, o-bay), from the dialect rendering of *che belli! che belli!* ('how beautiful'). Stalls sell regional foods, especially sweets, and seasonal handicrafts. To cater for the large crowds, it's been uprooted from Sant'Ambrogio's piazza and takes place in the grounds of Castello Sforzesco.

L'Artigiano in Fiera

www.artigianoinfiera.it/eng/

Huge craft fair for both trade and the public held at fieramilano (Rho).

La Scala Season Opening

www.teatroallascala.org/en/

Both the ballet and opera season begin on 7 December, also the Festa di Sant'Ambrogio. Tickets to the opening night of the opera are about as rare as countertenors; if you do strike it lucky, frocking up is obligatory (and part of the fun).

>ITINERARIES

Relax and unwind in the vast expanses of Parco Sempione (p92)

ITINERARIES

DAY ONE

Start your day with an early morning *cappuccio* and custard-filled brioche at the stone benches of Princi (p54), have a quick poke in Peck (p53) before climbing the stairs to the roof of the Duomo for a rare bird's-eye view of the city. Stroll down Galleria Vittorio Emanuele II, window shop at the original Prada shop (p50) then pass La Scala to Via Manzoni. Call into the Armani megastore then wander the streets of the Quadrilatero D'Oro. Depending on your shopping stamina, it may be time for a macchiato at Cova (p70). Wander down to Corso Venezia and continue browsing the interior showrooms. Make your way back to the Duomo via Corso Vittorio Emmanuele and have a late lunch at Obika (p53) on the top floor of Rinascente. Make your way to Castello Sforzesco down Via Dante, and stroll through the park to the Design Museum at the Triennale (p94). Get glammed up back at your hotel and make a grand *aperitivo* entrance at the Bulgari Hotel (p86), then hotfoot it to the opera at La Scala (p48). Have a post-show supper at the Trussardi Café (p51) or grab a *gianduia* (hazelnut/chocolate) gelati at Grom (p51).

DAY TWO

Head to Corso Magenta to see the Cenacolo (p21) or for the more mid-century minded, substitute the Studio Museo Achille Castiglioni (p92). Grab lunch and a beer at Bar Magenta and a *gelato* from Chocolat (p147) and trace the walls of Castello Sforzesco to Brera. Shop and wander the cobbled streets, ending up at the Pinocoteca. Have dinner at Pescheria da Claudio (p86) then make your way up to Corso Como for drinks.

DAY THREE

Wind your way down Via Torino from the Piazza del Duomo to Porta Ticenese for shopping, say *salve* to the columns of San Lorenzo then on to Navigli. Have lunch at a canalside *osteria* and discover the area's shops, then cross the bridge in Zona Tortona for more. Rest up with a drink at one of Navigli's bars then pop into a gallery opening, snaffle a pizza at Piccola Iscia (p124) before more drinks at Capetown (p137). Find yourself lipsyncing to Loredana Bertè at 2am at Plastic (p126).

Top Bergamo (p152) makes an appealing day-trip destination from Milan **Bottom left** Late afternoon is a great time to seek out some of Naviglio Grande's canalside bars (p19) **Bottom right** Window-shopping is always affordable in Via della Spiga (p68)

BUDGET

Stand for a coffee and *cornetto* (croissant; rarely more than €3), then find a street market and gather up provisions for lunch (and perhaps a pair of last season's Prada sandals). Visit the Galleria d'Arte Moderna (p62) and PAC (p64), kick a ball in the Giardini Pubblici, then feast on your picnic. Head to Corso Buenos Aires for a shopping buzz sans hefty price tags, then have a complimentary rest on an Antonio Citterio sofa at the B&B showroom (p113) on your way back to the centre. Take the tram to Living (p98), arriving early to make the most of the *aperitivo* spread – it's dinner. You'll have booked a Radiobus (p184) to pick you up for a night at Magazzini Generale (p126).

SUNDAY

Go to mass at the Duomo (p43), for booming bells and sublime early morning light through the stained-glass windows. Quick coffee and brioche before a blockbuster art show at the Palazzo Reale (p43), then a big brunch at Piquenique (p136). Browse the Navigli antique market (p19) or take the metro to San Siro for a football match. Finish the day with dinner at Dolce & Gabbana Gold (p118; open Sundays).

Milan has many street markets in almost every neighbourhood

FORWARD PLANNING

Three months before you go Book your tickets for the Cenacolo (p21) and opera or ballet performances at La Scala (p18); if you're visiting during Fashion Week or the Salone di Mobile, book accommodation and a car service.

Three weeks before you go Book a table at Cracco (p55) or Trussardi alla Scala (p55); rustle up tickets for the football (p26); arrange appointments for bespoke tailoring at E. Marinella (p144) or Tom Ford (p69), book a treatment at the Bulgari Spa (p87).

One week before you go Check out Start Milano (www.start-mi.net) for gallery openings; book your visit to the Museo Studio Achille Castiglioni (p92); make dinner bookings for all but the most casual of restaurants; check Zero (milano.zero.eu) for which bands will be in town; inspect your travel wardrobe and arrange dry cleaning, mending or last minute alterations, polish shoes (scruffy won't do).

The day before you go Get yourself on the guest list at Plastic's London Loves (p126); check the weather report at Corriere della Sera (meteo.corriere.it); do a juice fast in preparation for the pastry and *cotoletta* (veal cutlets) onslaught.

GREY DAY

Hot chocolates at Marchesi (p53), then pop into Rinascente for an umbrella and a Philosophy by Alberta Ferretti trench. Keep cosy with a tour of the city's beautiful house museums: Museos Poldi-Pezzoli (p63), Bagatti Valsecchi (p63), di Boschi-Stefano (p62) and the Villa Necchi-Campiglio (p22), with a liquid-led lunch at La Cantina di Manuela (p95) in between. Finish your day with a hearty risotto and *cotolletta* at Antica Tratoria della Pesa (p106) to ward off the chill.

>1	Around Duomo	42
>2	Quadrilatero D'Oro & Giardini Pubblici	58
>3	Brera	76
>4	Parco Sempione	88
>5	Corso Como, Porta Garibaldi & Isola	100
>6	San Babila	110
>7	Porta Romana & the South	120
>8	Navigli, Porta Ticenese & Zona Tortona	128
>9	Corso Magenta, Sant'Ambrogio & the West	140

Soak up the fun atmosphere on Milan's hippest shopping strip, Corso di Porta Ticinese (p128)

NEIGHBOURHOODS

Milan's big-city sprawl contains a tightly packed centre, crisscrossed spiderweb-style with ancient streets. Its runway-flat terrain and monumental buildings can make navigation tricky. Couple that with the seductive ease of the metro, and twigging to the city's simple layout can take a while. Milan is defined by concentric ring roads and radiating boulevards, while its ancient gates – Porta – act as compass points. Almost everything you'll want to see, do or buy is contained within the city's innermost circle.

The Milanese sometimes refer to numerical *zona* (zones), but more often, you'll hear a neighbourhood called by its nearest metro station, predominant street, or Porta. In this book we've captured a mix of them all.

The Duomo, the Galleria Vittorio Emanuele II, La Scala, as well as shops, restaurants and bars, cluster in the historic centre. The Quadrilatero D'Oro, the Golden Quad, is just northeast. Milan's famed luxury enclave has broken its rectangular boundaries to include Corso Venezia's southern end. Beyond here is the Giardini Pubblici, with an expanse of green and several museums. To the west of the Quad is Brera, a maze of cobblestone streets, low stucco buildings, shops, galleries, cafes and bars, plus the formidable collection of Renaissance painting. Parco Sempione is northwest, home to Castello Sforzesco, the Design Trienalle and around the Arco della Pace, bars. North, Brera blurs into shopping and nightlife-central Corso Como and Garibaldi. North across the train tracks is Isola, arty and independent. East is San Babila, with interior showrooms. Porta Romana, south, is an alternative nightlife spot while south of the centre, Porta Ticinese is where Milan's hipper kids come to shop and party. Navigli, the canal district and Zona Tortona is here too. Corso Magenta, home to the *Last Supper*, is west as is San Ambrogio, the cathedral and university neighbourhood.

CORSO COMO, PORTA GARIBALDI & ISOLA (p101)

QUADRILATERO D'ORO & GIARDINI PUBBLICI (pp60–1)

SAN BABILA (p111)

BRERA (pp78–9)

AROUND DUOMO (pp44–5)

PORTA ROMANA & THE SOUTH (p121)

PARCO SEMPIONE (pp90–1)

CORSO MAGENTA, SANT'AMBROGIO & THE WEST (p141)

NAVIGLI, PORTA TICINESE & ZONA TORTONA (p129)

0   0.5 miles
0   1 km

>AROUND DUOMO

Milan's centre is conveniently compact and, for the most part, free of cars. The splendid Duomo cathedral sits in a vast piazza, which throngs with tourists, touts and the Milanese themselves. From here, choose God or Mammon, art or music, or quickly take in all four: the Galleria Vittorio Emanuele II and Rinascente sit immediately to the side of the Duomo, La Scala or the galleries of the Piazza Reale are also a stroll away. Behind the piazza, Vie Spadari and Speorini secrete fabulous food shopping, stately Via Dante has a collection of midrange chains such as Petite Bateau and Sephora, and Via Torino and Corso Vittorio Emanuele pulse with *ragazzi* in a spending frenzy. Small shards of history can suddenly reveal themselves among the carrier-bags and Campari-sodas. Via Mercanti is the medieval core of the city, its palazzo built in 1228, while tucked away on Via Brisa, at the end of Via Meravigli, are the ruins of the Palace of Constantine, who gave imperial favour to Christianity in AD 313 from this very spot.

AROUND DUOMO

◎ SEE

Galleria Vittorio Emanuele II	1	E3
Il Duomo	2	E3
Museo del Duomo	3	E4
Palazzo Reale	4	E4
Pinacoteca & Biblioteca Ambrosiana	5	C4
San Bernardino alle Ossa	6	G4
Santa Maria presso San Satiro	7	D4
Teatro la Scala	8	D1
Teatro la Scala Museum	9	D2
Torre Velasca	10	E6

◎ SHOP

Borsolino	11	E2
Citta del Sole	12	C3
Ginger	13	A3

Hoepli International Bookstore	14	E2
Libreria Rizzoli	15	E2
Madina Milano	16	A3
Piumelli	17	E2
Prada	18	E2
Rinascente	19	E3
Venchi	20	D3

◎ EAT

Café Trussardi	21	D2
Cracco	22	C4
Fratelli Freni	23	D4
Grom	24	D2
Gucci Caffé	25	E3
Il Marchesino	26	D2
L'Antico Ristorante Boeucc	27	F1
Maio	(see 19)	
Marchesi	28	A3
Obika	(see 19)	

Pasticceria Giovanni Galli	29	D3
Peck	30	C4
Peck Italian Bar	31	C3
Princi	32	D4
Trussardi alla Scala Ristorante	(see 21)	

◎ DRINK

Caffé Zucca	33	E3
G-Lounge	34	F5
Straf Bar	35	E3

◎ PLAY

La Banque	36	C2
Piccolo Teatro (Teatro Grassi)	37	B2

Please see over for map

◉ SEE

◉ GALLERIA VITTORIO EMANUELE II

Piazza del Duomo; Ⓜ Duomo

So much more than a shopping arcade, the Galleria is known as *il salotto bueno*, the city's fine drawing room, and marks the *passiagiata* (passenger) route from Piazza di Duomo to Piazza di Marino to La Scala.

◉ IL DUOMO

Piazza del Duomo; Ⓜ Duomo

Milan's enduring symbol towers at its heart, pale, willowy and sublimely beautiful. Commissioned in 1386, its frenzy of flying buttresses, spires and statues took almost 500 years to complete.

The cathedral's echoing interior is equally stunning; its stained-glass windows and intricately carved pillars are worth braving the security checks for (and note, the skimpily dressed will not be admitted). The roof's forest of spires, statuary and pinnacles (and rare views of the city sprawl and Lombard plains) can be reached by 165 **steps** (admission €4; 🕓 9am-5.45pm) or a **lift** (admission €6; 🕓 9am-5.30pm). Entrances to both are on the cathedral's northern exterior. The **Museo del Duomo** (☎ 02 860358; www.duomomilano.it; Piazza del Duomo 14) was closed at time of research, check the Duomo's web-

The striking interior of Il Duomo

site for dates of an oft-promised reopening.

◉ PALAZZO REALE

☎ 02 875672; www.comune.milano.it /palazzoreale/; Piazza del Duomo 12; exhibitions €5-12, Museo della Reggia free; 🕓 exhibitions 2.30-5.30pm Mon, 9.30am-5.30pm Tue, Wed & Fri-Sun, 9.30am-10.20pm Thu, Museo 9.30am-5.30pm Tue-Sun; Ⓜ Duomo

Empress Maria Theresa's favourite architect Giuseppe Piermarini gave this old town hall and Visconti palace a neoclassical over-haul in the late 18th century. Its supremely elegant interiors were all but destroyed by WWII bombs; the Sala delle Cariatidi remains unrenovated as a grim reminder

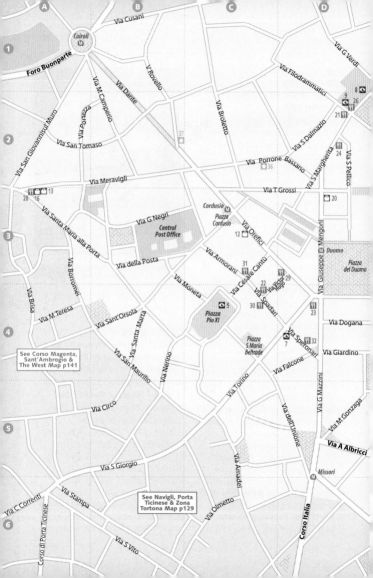

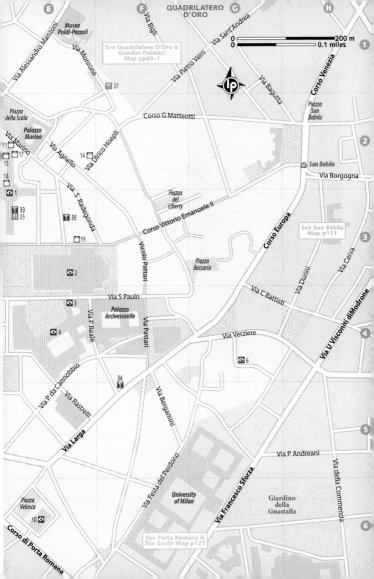

NEIGHBOURHOODS

AROUND DUOMO

of war's indiscriminate destruction. The palazzo has a small permanent art collection, but brings in the crowds with blockbuster shows from artists as diverse as Balla, Bacon and Vivienne Westwood.

☉ PINACOTECA & BIBLIOTECA AMBROSIANA

☎ 02 806921; www.ambrosiana.it; Piazza Pio XI 2; ☽ 9.30am-5pm Mon-Fri; Ⓜ Cordusio

Europe's first public library, the 1609-built Biblioteca Ambrosiana was once more about intellectual ferment than quiet scholarship. It houses 75,000 volumes and 35,000 manuscripts, while upstairs the **Pinacoteca Ambrosiana** (☎ 02 806921; www.ambrosiana.it; Piazza Pio XI 2; adult/concession €8/5; ☽ 10am-5.30pm Tue-Sun) has its fair share of breakthrough works including Caravaggio's *Canestra di Frutta* (Basket of Fruit), which helped launch the young painter's career and initiated Italy's ultrarealist tradition.

☉ SAN BERNARDINO ALLE OSSA

☎ 02 855 6304; Via San Bernardino; ☽ 7.30am-noon & 1-6pm Mon-Fri, 7.30am-12.30pm Sat, 9.30am-12.30pm Sun; ☐ 12, 15, 23, 27

Hidden down a corridor on the right of the main church, this small 17th-century ossuary has some bony rococo detailing, but most of the skulls, leg and arm bones are stacked to form creepy cruciform patterns.

☉ SANTA MARIA PRESSO SAN SATIRO

Via Speronari 3; ☽ 9am-noon & 2.30-6pm; Ⓜ Duomo

Here's an escape from the Zara/Benneton/H&M maelstrom. Ludovico Sforza saw potential in this little church built on top of the

Dario Fo

Nobel Laureate, theatre director & playwright, definitely not a moderate.

What is inspiring about Milan? It's a city that has lost its soul; it only remains on the face of postcards. What I can say is that I continue to love Milan despite everything. Even though Milan is no longer Milan. **Once Milan was considered the 'moral capital' of Italy; is that still the case?** I don't think that anyone could call it that now. It was, certainly, but in the past. It was a city for scientists and academics, painters and poets. It was a *città aperta*, an open city: alive and generous, offering work, culture, a home. A place of welcome and hope for thousands and thousands of immigrants. Where is that now? **What about theatre? Wasn't it once the city's conscience?** The theatres, especially the small, independent ones, are closing bit by bit. Historical spaces, like Teatro Lirico, have, scandalously, been closed for years. The fact is that the administrators of Milan are light years away from the theatre. You can't pretend to be a connoisseur of art if in life you're always playing the accountant. **During your 2006 Mayoral campaign, you said that Milan was profoundly broken; what's happened since then?** Very little has improved. One example is the Teatro Arcimboldi, the space out in Bicocca that temporarily housed La Scala. It's utterly desolate, it's been abandoned to itself. Because in Milan, the only law in force is that of the speculators. The Expo is now on the horizon, and it's a great opportunity to rise again. But that's not going to happen if the same old logic is applied. **What are your favourite corners of the city?** The little streets that open up behind the Duomo; the columns of San Lorenzo with the magnificent basilica; the Pinacoteca and Accademia Brera which still remain a splendid museum and a vital art school.

9th-century mausoleum of martyr San Satiro, and asked architect Donato Bramante to refurb in 1482. His ambition wasn't dampened by the project's scale: a trompe-l'oeil coffered niche on the shallow apse makes the backdrop to the altar mimic the Pantheon in Rome.

☎ TEATRO LA SCALA

☎ 02 88791, box office 02 861827; **www.teatroallascala.org**/ Via Filodrammatici 2; **M** Duomo

Milan's opera house normally only goes by one name – a true diva. A delicate shade of parchment yellow and austere on the outside, inside it's another story. This hallowed hall has had the world in thrall for more than two centuries; the recent grumbles over conservative rep productions and kerfuffling on musical directors pales into insignificance. Whether it's Puccini, a performance by dancer Roberto Bolle or cutting-edge choral or orchestral work, it's glorious. Yes, there is a dress code, tickets cost a bomb and need to be booked very well in advance.

☎ TEATRO LA SCALA MUSEUM

☎ 02 887 97 473; www.teatroallascala .org/ Largo Ghiringhelli 1, Piazza della Scala; adult/concession €5/4; ⏰ 9am-noon & 1.30-5pm; **M** Duomo

Harlequin costumes and a spinet inscribed with the command 'Inexpert hand, touch me not!' hint at centuries of Milanese musical drama, on and off stage. Portraits show Rossini apparently chatting up patrons, while Verdi seems troubled by mixed reviews, and Callas, ever the goddess, rises above it all. Your visit can include a glimpse of the theatre's famed interior from a box and a backstage tour if you don't clash with rehearsal time. The museum's **Livia Simoni Library** (☎ 02 46 912 49; Palazzo Busca, Corso Magenta) beckons buffs who want more.

☎ TORRE VELASCA

Piazza Velasca; **M** Missori

Studio BBPR's 1958 skyscraper outdoes '80s Memphis in the post-modern quoting stakes. The top-heavy tower campily tilts at Castello Sforzesco and the Duomo's lovely buttresses. Slightly sinister, ever so sci-fi and cleverly maximising use of available footprint, it's Lombard to the core. Sadly, apart from the foyer, it's currently as unbreachable as the medieval fortresses it emulates.

🛍 SHOPPING

🛍 BORSOLINO Hats

☎ 02 890 15 436; Galleria Vittorio Emanuele II 92; ⏰ 10am-7pm Tue-Sat; **M** Duomo

The iconic Alessandrian milliner has worked with the greats

(Achille Castiglioni once designed a pudding bowl bowler) and it still has room for whimsy as the feathery numbers attest. This little shop at the Galleria's Piazza Marino entrance is good for practical pitstops as well as nostalgic browsing and fantasy try ons.

CITTA DEL SOLE *Toys*
☎ 02 864 61 683; www.cittadelsole .it; Via Orefici 13; ⏱ 10am-7pm; Ⓜ Cordusio

Inspire your little Leonardo with that book on bridges designed by da Vinci or groom a mini Gae Aulenti with Bauhaus blocks.

GINGER *Antiques*
Via Meravigli 17; ⏱ 4.30-6.30pm Mon, 10.30am-1.30pm & 4.30-6.30pm Tue-Sat; Ⓜ Cordusio

This hole-in-the-wall antique store has a friendly owner who is happy to walk you through his wealth of treasures and curios, including a small treasured collection of Staffordshire.

HOEPLI INTERNATIONAL BOOKSTORE *Bookshop*
☎ 02 864871; www.hoepli.it; Via Ulrico Hoepli 5; ⏱ 10am-7.30pm Mon-Sat; Ⓜ Duomo

Italy's largest bookshop has six floors and some 500,000 titles and rare antiquarian books, as well as

an English- and German-language section. Don't neglect to browse the Italian shelves, even if you don't speak the language as local publishers are known for their beautiful cover design and innovative pictorial titles.

LIBRERIA RIZZOLI *Bookshop*
☎ 02 864 61 071; www.libreriariz zoli.it; Galleria Vittorio Emanuele II; ⏱ 9am-9pm Mon-Sat, 10am-8pm Sun; Ⓜ Duomo

The renowned art-book publisher also offers Italian literature and history in translation, plus great foreign newspapers, magazines and a full range of travel guides in English.

MADINA MILANO *Cosmetics*
☎ 02 869 15 438; www.madina.it; Via Meravigli 17; ⏱ 3.30-7.30pm Mon, 10am-7.30pm Tue-Sun; Ⓜ Cordusio

Madina is Milan's own cult cosmetic label. Complimentary makeovers let you experiment with the extraordinary range of colours and finishes.

PIUMELLI *Accessories*
☎ 02 869 2318; www.piumelli.com; Galleria Vittorio Emanuele II; ⏱ 10am-7pm Mon-Sat, 2-7pm Sun; Ⓜ Duomo

Leather gloves come in a huge range of styles, every colour of the rainbow and a choice of luxury linings (silk, cashmere, lapin). For

NEIGHBOURHOODS

AROUND DUOMO

those with either delicate digits or mighty man-hands, they have a full range of sizes and friendly staff to advise on fit. Look out for the sales baskets when not just after basic black.

🏬 PRADA *Fashion, Accessories*
☎ 02 876979; www.prada.com; Galleria Vittorio Emanuele II 63/65; 🕙 10am-7pm Mon-Sat, 2-7pm Sun; Ⓜ Duomo
The original Prada brothers leather and luggage shop is now the brand's flagship store and you can glimpse the past in the original till and black and white tiles. Downstairs, when confronted with the entire collection in one place, it feels as if you've slipped into an alternative universe, where there's Prada for every mood, and every mood is Prada.

🏬 RINASCENTE
Department store
☎ 02 88521; www.rinascente.it; Piazza Duomo; 🕙 10am-midnight; Ⓜ Duomo
Italy's most prestigious department store doesn't let the fashion capital down. Come for Italian diffusion lines, French lovelies and LA upstarts. (While it makes convenient one-stop shopping, there's a disturbing disjunct between the swirling department store frenzy and the superluxe price tags.) The basement hides an amazing homewares department (Guzzini

to iittala, and Italian-mama pots and pans for a steal) as well as a tax-back office for non-EU citizens. Up on the 7th floor, the Food Market will both feed you and tick gift to-buy souvenirs with its edible souvenirs, top-notch casual dining and gob-smacking views of the Duomo.

🍫 VENCHI *Chocolate*
☎ 02 890 96 178; www.venchi.it; Via Mengoni, Piazza Duomo; 🕙 10am-7pm Mon-Sat; Ⓜ Duomo
This Piedmontese chocolatier has basic blocks, highly original products including 'chocavier' (90% cocoa granules), cocoa dusted *fave* (beans) and truffle cigars. Be warned: it just takes one smear of their gianduja cream spread and there's no going back to Nutella.

🍴 EAT

🍴 CAFFÉ GUCCI *Cafe*   €
☎ 02 859 79 932; Galleria Vittorio Emanuele II 11; 🕙 10am-7pm Mon-Sat, 2-7pm Sun; Ⓜ Duomo
This terrace addition to the Gucci shop offers the best people-perving in the middle of the Galleria (McDonald's aside), with heating in the cooler months. The chocolates to go with your espresso bear the house double-Gs, for brand-amnesiacs.

🍴 CAFÉ TRUSSARDI
Contemporary Italian €€

☎ 02 806 88 295; www.trussardi
allascala.it; Piazza della Scala 5;
🕐 7.30am-11pm Mon-Fri, 9am-11pm
Sat; Ⓜ Duomo

Whether it's for a glass of wine and root vegetable crisps at the bar, or a leisurely meal from a small, changing menu beneath Patrick Blanc's beautiful vertical garden in the courtyard, this is one of Milan's most stylish, low-key dining options.

🍴 FRATELLI FRENI *Pasticceria* €
☎ 02 877072; www.pasticceriafreni.com;
Via Torino 1, Piazza Duomo; 🕐 9am-
7.30pm Mon-Fri, 10am-7.30pm Sat & Sun;
Ⓜ Duomo

This pasticceria arrived with the first waves of southern immi-grants and continues to be a welcome splash of Sicilian colour right in Milan's centre. Potted prickly pears to smallgoods get the surreal marzipan treatment. Photogenic as the marzipan madness is, a ricotta canoli delivers a *mezzogiorno* (midday) jolt without the sugar overload.

🍴 GROM *Gelateria* €
☎ 02 805 81 041; www.grom.it;
Via Santa Margherita 16; 🕐 11am-
11pm; Ⓜ Duomo

This Torinese chain's gentle attempt at world domination (there are branches on Broadway and Bleecker) is no reason to dismiss its wares. The pale and fragrant pistachio is made from nuts sourced from the slopes of Etna, a rich gianduja mixes roasted

Enjoy a low-key drink at Café Trussardi

NEIGHBOURHOODS

AROUND DUOMO

COFFEE SPEAK

un caffé single, strong shot of coffee, an espresso

caffé doppio two shots of the above

caffé lungo a shot with a dash of hot water

Americano a long black; as the name implies, a foreign concept

macchiato an espresso 'stained' with a dash of milk, either *caldo* (hot) or *freddo* (cold)

cappuccio a cappuccino, only to be ordered for breakfast

marocchino uniquely Milanese, a small, cocoa-topped cappuccino (incredibly, 'little Moroccan')

caffé latte a joke amount of coffee in a large cup of milk, for children

cappuccino Hag decaf cappuccino (pronounced 'arg', a brand name)

caffé corretto an espresso 'corrected' with a shot of grappa

Piedmontese hazelnuts with Venezuelan chocolate, and all sorbets and granita come from organic, seasonal fruit. Don't be afraid to ask for a taste, and do upgrade to Battifollo biscotti in lieu of spoons.

🍴 IL MARCHESINO
Contemporary Italian €€€
☎ 02 720 94 338; Via Filodrammatici 2; 🕑 7.30-1am Mon-Sat, kitchen closes 11pm; Ⓜ Duomo

Gualtiero Marchesi, Italy's most revered chef, presides over a modern dining room in that other Milanese institution, La Scala. Chairs upholstered in deep crimson evoke the neighbouring concert hall, as do musical notes cascading across white china. The menu is similarly traditional but infused with a creative spirit. Earthy handcut spaghetti is served with mussels and a verdant tangle of zucchini, foie-gras-scented roast pigeon is scattered with pinenuts and raisins atop the freshest baby spinach.

🍴 L'ANTICO RISTORANTE BOEUCC *Italian* €€€
☎ 02 760 20 224; www.boeucc.com; Piazza Belgioioso 2; 🕑 noon-2.30pm & 6-11pm Mon-Fri, 6-11pm Sat & Sun; Ⓜ Montenapoleone

You don't come to Milan's oldest restaurant looking for culinary innovation; when the menu strays from *cotoletto* to osso bucco it's to brains and zucchini flowers or roast goat with artichokes. A favourite with financiers from over the border, who don't need to be seen, it's tucked away in a pretty piazza overlooking the house of Alessandro Manzoni.

🍴 MAIO
Contemporary Italian €€
☎ 02 885 2455; Piazza Duomo, La Rinascente, 7th fl; 🕑 10am-midnight; Ⓜ Duomo

With the Duomo as a backdrop, a glass ceiling and a scattering of classic Eames chairs and Bertoia bar stools, the menu at this 7th-floor restaurant is a simple, tasty bonus. The *riso venere* (creamy black rice) with crab, salmon eggs and peas pleases all the senses, and pasta dishes, such as a squid ink ravioli, are far from timid. Maio does pizzas and club sandwiches too.

🍴 MARCHESI *Pasticceria*   €
☎ 02 876730; www.pasticceriamarchesi .it; Via Santa Maria alla Porta 11a; 🕑 8am-8pm Tue-Sat, 8am-1pm Sun; Ⓜ Cairoli, Cordusio

This wood-panelled pasticceria has been baking since 1824. The window displays have the wonky logic of a Hitchcock dream sequence but with perfect every-shot coffee,

there's no shock ending. Don't overlook the fruit gels packaged together in smartly contrasting fla-vours like green apple and prune.

🍴 OBIKA *Mozzarella bar*   €€
☎ 02 885 2453; www.obika.it; Via Santa Radegonda 3, La Rinascente Duomo 7th fl; 🕑 10am-midnight; Ⓜ Duomo

Rinascente's bustling branch of Brera's Obika (p85) gets you a close-up view of the Duomo's spires.

🍴 PECK *Food, Wine*
☎ 02 802 3161; www.peck.it; Via Spadari 9; 🕑 3.30-7.30pm Mon, 9.15am-7.30pm Tue-Sat; Ⓜ Duomo

Gourmet may have gone main-stream, but this multifloored food hall has been stocking Milanese

Take your pick at Marchesi

ECOPASSING

Milan's city council, the Comune di Milano, introduced the trial Ecopass in January 2008, in an attempt to combat the city's horrific traffic congestion and disastrous air pollution. Any car entering the designated central zone between 7am to 7pm Monday to Friday must display a Europass ticket. The prices vary from €2 to €10 depending on the Euro category pollution rating of what you're driving. Licence plate classifications are listed on the Ecopass website (you're exempt if your home country doesn't enforce the system, or confused if it does). The Europass can be bought online or from ATM shops, *tabacchi* and newsagents. The scheme goes on holiday with the rest of Milan in August.

Early reports showed a promising rise in the number of metro commuters, though, not so reassuringly, ongoing rates of noxious emissions were high enough for Milan to be declared the most polluted city in Europe several months after the scheme's introduction. Debate continues as to whether Ecopass is a step in the right direction or simply a token gesture to conform to EU directives. For more information contact **Ecopass** (☎ 02 02 02; www.comune .milano.it/ecopass); an English factsheet can be downloaded from the Italian-language site.

pantries for more than a century, and remains one of the world's most enticing. Its size won't overwhelm, but the range and quality of cheeses, oils, cured meats, chocolates, pastries, pasta and fresh produce will. Upstairs, the lunch bar with its pastel pink-clothed tables, wicker chairs and retro menu is like something out of a Lucio Binetti music vid from the early '80s, but is handy if observing the mantra 'never food shop hungry'. Don't miss the downstairs wine cellar on the way out.

🍽 PECK ITALIAN BAR
Italian   €€€
☎ 02 8693017; www.peck.it; Via Cesare Cantù 3; ⏱ 7.30am-8.30pm Mon-Sat; Ⓜ Duomo

Peck's dining room lets quality produce shine with staples like *cotoletto*, risotto and roasts done with fabulously fresh, well-sourced ingredients, if not a smidgen of contemporary flair. The room too is a picture of restraint, with wines by the glass administered by bow-tied waiters.

🍽 PRINCI *Bakery, Pasticceria*   €
☎ 02 874797; www.princi.it; Via Speronari 6; ⏱ 7am-8pm Mon-Fri, 8am-8pm Sat; Ⓜ Duomo
The minimalist design of this narrow cavelike space highlights the elements of bread – flour, water, fire – and the art of baking. Equally delicious for early morning *cornetto* or Stracchino-filled focaccia on the way home

at midnight. In between, do a standing-room only locals lunch: rare roast beef and parmesan-laced vegies or salmon steaks and radicchio salad.

🍽 CRACCO

Contemporary Italian €€€

☎ 02 876774; Via Victor Hugo 4; ⏰ 7.30-10.30pm Mon, 12.30-7.30pm Tue-Fri, 7.30-10.30pm Sat; Ⓜ Duomo

Despite the split with paternal Peck, baby-faced charmer Carlo Cracco can seemingly do no wrong as the Milanese lap up signature dishes like salt and sugar marinated eggs with as-paragus puree, a salad of intensely flavoured seafood 'leaves' and a risotto of Szechuan pepper, ginger and anchovies. Cracco's thoughtful, deconstructive style may polarise, though it's rarely as shocking as others from the Ferran Adriâ cabal; this is Italy after all.

🍽 TRUSSARDI ALLA SCALA RISTORANTE

Contemporary Italian €€€

☎ 02 806 88 201; www.trussardiallascala .it; Piazza della Scala 5; ⏰ closed Sat lunch & Sun; Ⓜ Duomo

Gualtiero Marchesi alumni, Andrea Berton, runs the kitchen in

Check out the stylish interior at Cracco

this subdued, sexy dining room, with windows looking out onto La Scala. The Trussardi touch is a light one; the parquetry and leather combo is far from stuffy. The food too has a directness, with seasonal dishes like grilled scallops with ginger powder and peanut cream or roast spring lamb with potato, avocado and lime, mixing it up with earthier Milanese favourites.

🍴 PASTICCERIA GIOVANNI GALLI *Pasticceria* €

☎ 02 864 64 833; www.giovannigalli.com; Via Victor Hugo 2; 🕑 8.30am-8pm Mon-Sat, 8.30am-2pm Sun; Ⓜ Duomo

Apparently, heaven can be purchased (at a price). *Alchechengi* are Lombard cherry tomatoes dunked in maraschino liquor and bitter chocolate. Since 1880, Milanese have salivated over the *marrons glacés* (candied chestnuts) in Galli's wooden display cases, but try the hello-new-world hot-pepper chocolates too.

🍸 DRINK

🍸 CAFFÉ ZUCCA *Cafe*

☎ 02 864 64 435; www.caffemiani.it; Galleria Vittorio Emanuele II 21; 🕑 lunch & dinner; Ⓜ Duomo

Linger over a midmorning cappuccio here or opt for a Campari soda and a dish of fat green olives or panini later in the day. Better to feast on some history rather than some of the often mediocre mains.

🍸 G-LOUNGE *Bar, Club*

☎ 02 805 3042; www.glounge.it; Via Larga 8; 🕑 7.30am-9.30pm Mon, 7.30-2am Tue-Sun; Ⓜ Duomo

By day, this former Fascist hangout/billiard hall does lunches with a view of the Torre Velasca; by night it's caipirinhias and chill-out tunes. Some call G-Lounge a straight-friendly gay bar, others a gay-friendly straight bar. We just call it fun.

🍸 STRAF BAR *Bar*

☎ 02 805 00 715; www.straf.it; Via San Raffael 3; 🕑 8am-midnight; Ⓜ Duomo

Pick of the centre's hotel bars with a busy nightly *aperitivo* scene that kicks on until pumpkin hour. The decor is along the now familiar mod-exotic lines: wood/metal/stone played up against minimalist concrete.

⭐ PLAY

⬛ LA BANQUE *Club*

☎ 02 869 96 565; Via Porrone Bassano 6; 🕑 6pm-2am Tue-Thu, 6pm-4am Fri & Sat, 7pm-midnight Sun; Ⓜ Cordusio

Ties and tongues get progressively looser as happy hour devolves into dinner – and once the dance floor posing kicks in, you never know where they'll end up. Don't worry, the Tamara de Lempicka-like ladies decorating the walls look like they want to kill the DJ too.

⭐ **PICCOLO TEATRO (TEATRO GRASSI)** *Theatre*
☎ **02 723 33 222; www.piccoloteatro .org; Via Rovello 2;** ⏲ **box office 10am-6.45pm Mon-Sat, 1-6.30pm Sun;** Ⓜ **Cordusio**

This risk-taking little repertory theatre was opened in 1947 by Paolo Grassi and none other than the late, great theatre direc-tor Giorgio Strehler, and then embarked on a nationwide move-ment of avant-garde productions and Commedia dell'Arte revivals. Additional programming, includ-ing ballet, goes on at the larger, second sibling space over at the Teatro Strehler (p87).

>QUADRILATERO D'ORO & GIARDINI PUBBLICI

Just northeast of the Duomo, the Quadrilatero D'Oro – the Golden Quad – sings a siren song to luxury label lovers the world over. It also goes by the diminutives Monte Nap or Napo after Via Monte Napoleone, which is one of its defining four streets along with Via della Spiga, Via Sant' Andrea and Via Borgospesso. Beyond the quad itself, Via Manzoni, Via Bagutta, Corso Matteotti, Via Verri and Corso Venezia are also now considered very shiny, if not golden. The latter continues northeast alongside the splendid Giardini Pubblici, home to notable galleries and museums. The area also boasts stunning residential architecture from 16th-century townhouses to towering Liberty-style apartment buildings. The neoclassical Porta Venezia – the gate facing Venice – and its surrounds are all rather grand too. Further north, Corso Buenos Aires is far more workaday, with a bustling energy and crowds of young Milanese shopping its kilometres of shops. The area around Piazza Lima is increasingly becoming a destination too, its elegant streets home to an ecclectic mix of ethnic restaurants and fashionable bars.

QUADRILATERO D'ORO & GIARDINI PUBBLICI

◉ SEE

Casa Museo Boschi
  di Stefano...................1 F2
Galleria d'Arte Moderna ..2 C4
Galleria Gió Marconi.......3 E2
Galleria Raffaella
  Cortese 4 G2
Galleria Tega 5 B4
Giardini Pubblici............6 C4
Museo Bagatti
  Valsecchi 7 B5
Museo Poldi-Pezzoli 8 A6
Padiglione d'Arte
  Contemporanea 9 C4
Planetario Ulrico
  Hoepli.......................10 D4
Spazio Oberdan............11 D3
Studio Guenzani............12 G4
Torre Rasini 13 E4

◉ SHOP

A+M Bookshop 14 F2
Alberta Ferretti............15 B6
Alberto Aspesi.............16 B6
Aprica 17 B5
Bottega del Cashmere..18 B5
Car Shoe 19 C6
Costume National 20 C6
Daad Dantone..............21 B5
DMagazine 22 B5
Dolce & Gabbana.........(see 72)
Dolce & Gabbana
  Accessories................23 C6

Dolce & Gabbana
  Boutique Donna.......24 C5
Driade.........................25 B5
DSquared....................26 B6
Emilio Pucci.................27 B6
Ermenegildo Zegna......28 B5
Etro.............................29 B6
Etro Profumi................30 B6
Fendi...........................31 C5
G Lorenzi 32 B6
Gallo...........................33 A5
Gianfranco Ferré ....(see 73)
Giorgio Armani............34 B5
Gucci...........................35 B6
Habits Culti..................36 D5
I Pinko Palino 37 B5
Iris..............................38 B6
Jil Sander....................39 B6
Marni...........................40 B5
Missoni 41 B6
Miu Miu 42 C5
Moschino.....................43 C6
Muji.............................44 F2
Paul Smith...................45 B5
Prada...........................46 B6
Roberto Cavalli............47 B5
Tom Ford 48 B6
Trussardi.....................49 C5
Valentino.....................50 B5
Versace 51 B6
Viktor & Rolf................52 C6
Wannenes il
  XX Secolo..................53 A5

▤ EAT

Armani Nobu................54 B5
Caffé Cova 55 B6
Don Carlos...................56 A5
Emporio Armani Caffè...57 A5
Il Baretto al Baglioni....58 C5
Il Salumaio
  Montenapoleone 59 B6
Il Teatro......................60 B5
Joia 61 D3
Piccola Ischia...............62 F2
Pizzeria Spontini..........63 G1
Trattoria di Giannino....64 C1
Warsa 65 F4

▼ DRINK

Bar Basso....................66 H3
Diana Garden...............67 E4
Just Cavalli Café 68 C5
L'Elephante..................69 F4
Lino's Coffee...............70 D5
Martini Bar ....(see 72)

☆ PLAY

Armani Privé 71 B5
Dolce & Gabbana
  Beauty Farm.............72 C6
E'SPA at Gianfranco
  Ferré 73 C5
Spa Guerlain at
  Hotel Baglioni ....(see 58)

Please see over for map

◉ SEE

◉ CASA MUSEO BOSCHI-DI STEFANO

☎ 02 202 40 568; 2nd fl, Via Jan 15; admission free; ⏲ 2-6pm Wed-Sun; Ⓜ Lima

Milan's best collection of 20th-century Italian painting is not proudly displayed in a purpose-built soaring white box. Somewhat tellingly, it's crowded salon-style in a Piero Portaluppi–designed 1930s apartment that still has the appearance of the haute-bourgeois home it once was. It's a heady art hit, with Boccioni's dynamic brushstrokes propelling painting towards Futurism, the nostalgically metaphysical Campigli and De Chirico, and the restless, expressionist Informels all occupying a small space. Don't miss the double-header of *concetti spaziali* (specialist experiments) from Milan's most important midcentury artists Fontana and Manzoni. The provocative slashed canvases of Fontana hang side by side with Manzoni's surface-busting *Anchromes*.

◉ GALLERIA D'ARTE MODERNA

GAM; ☎ 02 760 02 819; Via Palestro 16; ⏲ 9am-5.30pm Tue-Sun; Ⓜ Palestro

Napoleon's Milanese home, the 18th-century Villa Reale, now houses a museum of 19th- and early 20th-century Italian art, from neoclassical sculptor Canova to Futurist painters Balla and Boccioni (with some sickly Divisionists somewhere in between). Upstairs there is an impressive collection of the mythic-Modern sculptures of Marino Marini.

◉ GALLERIA GIÓ MARCONI

☎ 02 294 04 373; www.giomarconi.com; Via Tadino 15; ⏲ 10am-1pm & 4-8pm Tue-Sat (limited hr in summer); Ⓜ Lima

Gio Marconi shows a diverse range of work including celeb-obsessed Francesco Vezzoli, the highly conceptual Elisa Sighicelli, architectural drawings from the late neorationalist architect Aldo Rossi and neo-expressionist Tal R.

Wander through the Galleria d'Arte Moderna

◉ GALLERIA RAFFAELLA CORTESE

☎ 02 204 3555; www.galleriaraffaella cortese.com; Via Stradella 7; ⏱ 3-7.30pm Tue-Sat & by appointment; Ⓜ Lima

In a quiet street and down a steep driveway, this elongated basement space shows investigative, though amusing, work. Cortese's stable of artists includes locals like Michael Fliri and international names like Czech Jana Sterbak, Australian Destiny Deacon, New York–based Roni Horn and Kiki Smith.

◉ GALLERIA TEGA

☎ 02 760 06 473; www.galleriatega.it; Via Senato 24; ⏱ 10am-1pm & 3-7pm Mon-Fri; Ⓜ Montenapoleone

If you're in the market for a precious work on paper, this is a good place to browse the stock room. The family behind this gallery has been dealing art since 1939 and sources paintings, sculptures and other pieces from Europe's 20th-century greats.

◉ GIARDINI PUBBLICI

⏱ 6.30am-sunset; Ⓜ Palestro

A life story unfolds as you follow pebble paths past bumper cars and a carousel, onward past a game of kick to kick, kissing teens, a beer kiosk, baby prams, jogging paths and shady benches. Jump in, or just stop and smell the roses.

For grey days the charming **Museo Civico di Storia Naturale** (Natural History Museum; ☎ 02 884 63 280; Corso Venezia, 55; adult/concession €3/1.50; ⏱ 9am-5.30pm Tue-Sun) beckons, the grand neo-Romanesque building houses dinosaurs, fossils and the largest geology collection in Europe.

◉ MUSEO BAGATTI VALSECCHI

☎ 02 760 06 132; www.museobagatti valsecchi.org; Via Gesù 5; admission €6, Wed €3; ⏱ 1-5.45pm Tue-Sun; Ⓜ Montenapoleone

Though born a few centuries too late, the Bagatti Valsecchi brothers were determined to be Renaissance men, and from 1878 to 1887 built their home as a living museum of the Quattrocento.

◉ MUSEO POLDI-PEZZOLI

☎ 02 794889; Via Alessandro Manzoni 12; admission €6/4; ⏱ 10am-6pm Tue-Sun; Ⓜ Montenapoleone

Giacomo Poldi-Pezzoli, blessed with a fortune, aristocratic connections and an obsessive streak, managed to amass an amazing collection of Renaissance treasures during his short lifetime. Inspired by the 'house museum' that was later to become London's V&A, he got busy transforming his apartment into a series of historically styled rooms. Treasures include Pollaiuolo's profile of a woman, despite the beautifully detailed strings of

A tram passes the palazzo that houses Museo Poldi-Pezzoli (p63)

pearly conspicuous consumption, arrestingly intimate and oddly domestic.

PADIGLIONE D'ARTE CONTEMPORANEA

PAC; ☎ 02 760 09 085; www.comune .milano.it/pac; Via Palestro 14; admission free depending on exhibition; 9.30am-5.30pm Tue-Fri, 9.30am-7pm Sat & Sun; M Palestro

Built in 1954 on the site of the Palazzo Reale's stables that were destroyed by WWII bombs, the PAC was one of Milan's most significant examples of midcentury architecture. It was itself destroyed by a Mafia bomb in 1993 and its rebuilding in 1996 was quixotically faithful to the original; curatorial vision now strains against space

limitations. The shows at this Kunsthall, especially international collaborations, can be daring, but rarely reflect the dynamism of the local scene.

PLANETARIO ULRICO HOEPLI

☎ 02 295 31 181; www.comune.milano.it /planetario; Corso Venezia 57; admission €3/1.50; M Palestro

Rationalist Piero Portaluppi let his neoclassical side rip with this 1930 planetarium built for publisher Ulrico Hoepli. It's a wonderfully quaint and charming thing, and most likely your only chance to see stars in Milan. Ring to check for opening hours as it's a favoured spot for functions (ie fashion shows).

◉ SPAZIO OBERDAN
☎ 02 774 06 300; www.cinetecamilano.it;
Viale Vittorio Veneto 2; ⏲ **10am-7.30pm Tue-Sun, 10am-10pm Thu & Fri;**
Ⓜ **Porta Venezia**
The riches of Milan's *Cineteca* (cinematheque, or film library) are screened downstairs, while upstairs there's a programme of exhibitions from stills to video art. The original cinema was redesigned by architect Gae Aulenti, better known for her work on Cadorna station and Paris' Musée d'Orsay.

◉ STUDIO GUENZANI
☎ 02 294 09 251; www.studioguenzani.it;
Via Bartolomeo Eustachi 10; ⏲ **3-7.30pm Tue-Fri;** Ⓜ **Lima**
Shows here are from an excellent stable of Italian artists (such as Arte Povera–influenced Stefano Arienti) to international luminaries like Yasumasa Morimura and Cindy Sherman.

◉ TORRE RASINI
Corso Venezia 61; Ⓜ **Porta Venezia**
This squat block clad in the smoothest white marble and dark, textured tower were designed by Gio Ponti and Emilio Lancia in 1934. The odd pairing is indicative of the tension going on between the Novecento and Rationalist architectural styles.

SHOP

◉ A+M BOOKSHOP
Bookshop
☎ 02 295 27 729; www.artecontemporanea.com; Via Tadino 30; ⏲ **11am-1pm & 3.30-7.30pm Tue-Sat;** Ⓜ **Lima**
Contemporary art monographs, catalogues and audiovisual material join gorgeously realised a+m edizioni titles that cover an inspiringly diverse range of artists and theorists as well as thoughtful visual essays on everything from New York's community gardens to the reconstruction of Milan's PAC.

◉ APRICA
Children's wear, Accessories
☎ 02 760 25 850; www.aprica-montenapo.com; Via Monte Napoleone 27; ⏲ **10am-1.30pm & 2.30-7pm Tue-Fri, 10am-7pm Sat;**
Ⓜ **Montenapoleone**
Aprica's *passeginas* (strollers) raise the style stakes way beyond Bugaboo, sprouting exquisite organza-leaved boot covers in grownup shades of mushroom or ink. For little label slaves, there's special edition bibs, the linked Fendi Fs awaiting their first slop.

◉ ASPESI *Fashion*
☎ 02 760 22 478; www.aspesi.it;
Via Montenapoleone 13; ⏲ **10am-7pm Mon-Sat;** Ⓜ **Montenapoleone**
The size of this Antonio Citterio–designed shop is a clue to just how much Italians love this label;

DYNASTY, ITALIAN STYLE: MILAN'S FIRST FAMILIES OF FASHION

Etro Milanese papa Gimmo still heads up the firm, with siblings Jacopo, Ippolito and Veronica on the payroll, though creative director Kean gets all the attention (shocking declarations about liking the smell of earth and wearing shirts to bed *and* the next day make news in Italy).

Gucci *The House of Gucci* tells the torrid story of the Florentine family, including the 1995 assassination of Maurizio in front of his Milan apartment, by his exwife.

Missoni Knitwear innovators Rosita and Tai started out in 1948 and she still designs homewares; kids Luca, Angela, and Vittorio oversee the fashion side of the business while photogenic grandchildren accompany *nonna* and *nonno* to openings and parties (even aspiring actress Margherita keeps it tidy).

Prada Muicca ('Mrs Prada' to staff) and husband Patrizio Bertelli have a famously fiery relationship, but together have turned her grandfather's luggage business into a household name (and put themselves on the Forbes Rich List); whether teenage sons step up is yet to be seen.

Trussardi Bergamaschi glovemaker Dante Trussardi's grandson Nicola went on to create a global luxury brand, but the family has suffered terrible tragedy; first Nicola then four years later son, and new CEO, Francesco were killed in car crashes, leaving daughter Beatrice to carry on.

Versace The ultimate Calabrian boy made good, Gianni was murdered outside his Miami villa; sister Donatella keeps the brand buoyant while niece and heir Allegra Beck battles anorexia.

Aspesi outerwear is *de rigueur* for mountain and lake weekends. The arty industrial sprawl is ironically at odds with an essentially practical marque: sportswear at its most understated.

🔲 BOTTEGA DEL CASHMERE
Fashion

☎ 02 798711; Via Alessandro Manzoni 46; 🕑 10am-1pm & 2.30-7pm Mon-Sat; Ⓜ Montenapoleone
Lovely individual shop with an extensive range of quality

cashmere. (Some of us are too sensitive to wear ordinary wool.)

🔲 CAR SHOE *Shoes*

☎ 02 760 24 027; www.carshoe.com; Via Della Spiga 1; 🕑 10am-7.30pm Mon-Sat, 11am-7pm Sun; Ⓜ Montenapoleone
Now under the wing of Patrizio Bertelli (Mr Prada), the original '60s hybrid of sport shoe and smart casual loafer is set for a comeback in this flagship shop. To counter the lothario rep, it now also does ranges for women and kids.

◻ DAAD DANTONE *Fashion*
☎ 02 760 16 045; www.daad-dantone.com; Via Santo Spirito 24a; ◷ 10am-7pm Mon-Sat; Ⓜ Montenapoleone

This beautiful shop creates a stir with its collection of edgy Japanese and European labels and designer collaborations. The arresting window displays facing Via della Spiga are always worth a look.

◻ DMAGAZINE *Fashion, Outlet*
☎ 02 760 06 027; http://dmagazine.it; Via Montenapoleone 26; ◷ 9.30am-7.45pm; Ⓜ Montenapoleone

Given you usually have to schlep out of town for deeply discounted designer threads, what's up with this perversely central outlet? Yes, all the major labels are here, but tend to be the stranger of their kind. Plus the tawdry jumble of oddments still going for many hundreds of euro and a barely contained atmosphere of frenzy can make even the most dedicated fashionista sick at heart.

◻ DRIADE *Furniture, Design*
☎ 02 760 20 359; www.driade.com; Via Manzoni 30; ◷ 10am-7pm Tue-Fri, 3-7pm Mon; Ⓜ Montenapoleone

Frescoed rooms present the ultimate design challenge – with all those cherubim flying around, suddenly that houndstooth sofa seems a bit too much – but Driade rises to the occasion in its own converted neoclassical palazzo with impeccable eclecticism, unconventional materials and top international designers.

◻ G LORENZI
Homewares, Design
☎ 02 760 22 848; Via Monte Napoleone 9; ◷ 3-7.30pm Mon, 9am-12.30pm & 3-7.30pm Tue-Sat; Ⓜ Montenapoleone

One of Milan's extant early 20th-century gems, G Lorenzi specialises in the finest quality grooming, kitchen and general paraphernalia from pure-bristled handmade brushes to specialist knives and walking sticks.

◻ GALLO *Fashion, Accessories*
☎ 02 783602; www.gallospa.it; Via Manzoni 16; ◷ 10am-7pm; Ⓜ Montenapoleone

Gallo may spice up its seasonal collections but it's the perennial striped knee-socks that locals love for adding secret colour to drab business attire. The range for men, women, children and babes is as equally wide. You'll never risk losing these beauties in the dryer, especially at €12 to €35 a pop.

HABITS CULTI
Homewares, Fashion
☎ 02 780637; www.habitsculti.it;
Corso Venezia 53; ⏰ 10am-7pm
Mon-Sat; Ⓜ Palestro
Culti's pared-back minimalist homewares retain a tactile earthiness. The range of linen placemats, blond-wood kitchen implements, room fragrances and crumpled tunics can prove addictive – next thing you'll be holed up at its Puglian resort and not taking calls.

DESIGNER CHECKLIST

The Quad's designer bounty is so great that it precludes individual listings. Below are all the big names; most open 10am to 7pm Monday to Saturday.

Alberta Ferretti (☎ 02 760 22 780; Via Monte Napoleone 21)

Costume National (☎ 02 760 18 356; Via Sant'Andrea 12)

Dolce & Gabbana (☎ 02 760 01 155; Via della Spiga & Corso Venezia 15; ☎ 02 778831; Corso Venezia 15 & Via Spiga 2)

DSquared (☎ 02 896 91 699; Via Pietro Verri 4)

Emilio Pucci (☎ 02 763 18 356; Via Monte Napoleone 14)

Ermenegildo Zegna (☎ 02 760 06 437; Via Monte Napoleone 27)

Etro (☎ 02 760 05 049; Via Monte Napoleone 5)

Etro Profumi (☎ 02 760 05 450; Via Verri, cnr Via Bigli)

Fendi (☎ 02 760 21 617; Via Sant'Andrea 16)

Gianfranco Ferré (☎ 02 783050; Via Della Spiga 7; ☎ 02 780406; Via Sant'Andrea 15)

Giorgio Armani (☎ 02 723 18 600; Via Alessandro Manzoni 31)

Gucci (☎ 02 771271; Via Monte Napoleone 5-7)

Jil Sander (☎ 02 777 2991; Via Pietro Verri 6)

Marni (☎ 02 763 17 327; Via della Spiga 50)

Missoni (☎ 02 760 03 555; Via Monte Napoleone 8)

Miu Miu (☎ 02 760 01 799; Via Sant'Andrea 21)

Moschino (☎ 02 760 00 832; Via Sant'Andrea 12)

Prada (☎ 02 777 1771; Monte Napoleone 6; Via Sant'Andrea 21; Via Spiga 1 & 5)

Roberto Cavalli (☎ 02 760 20 900; Via della Spiga 42; ☎ 02 763 16 566; Via della Spiga 30)

Trussardi (☎ 02 806 88 242; Piazza della Scala 5; ☎ 02 760 20 380; Via Sant'Andrea 3)

Valentino (☎ 02 760 06 182; Via Monte Napoleone 20)

Versace (☎ 02 760 08 528; Via Monte Napoleone 11; ☎ 02 760 13 871; Via Gesu 12)

Viktor & Rolf (☎ 02 796 091; Via Sant'Andrea 14)

☐ I PINKO PALINO
Children's wear

☎ 02 781931; Via della Spiga 42 & Via Borgospesso 25; ⏱ 10am-7pm Mon-Sat; Ⓜ Montenapoleone

Enchanted parents surrender small fortunes here on hand-sewn floating silk dresses and whimsically embroidered overalls. Outfits can be fully accessorised, as you'd expect from Italy's most beautiful children's label.

☐ IRIS *Shoes*

☎ 02 799988; Via Sant'Andrea 10; ⏱ 10am-2pm & 3-7pm Mon-Sat; Ⓜ Montenapoleone

Those in the know head to Iris to snap up not-so-easy to find footwear from edgier under-license labels John Galliano, Proenza Schouler, Veronique Branquinho and Viktor & Rolf.

☐ MUJI *Homewares, Fashion*

☎ 02 742 81 169; www.muji.net; Corso Buenos Aires 36; ⏱ noon-7.30pm Mon & Sun, 10.30am-7.30pm Tue-Sat; Ⓜ Lima

Escape the Corso Buenos Aires visual vortex for Muji monochrome and the serenity of a logo-less life.

☐ PAUL SMITH *Fashion*

☎ 02 763 19 181; Via Alessandro Manzoni 30; ⏱ 10am-7pm Mon-Sat; Ⓜ Montenapoleone

Smith's pink palazzo is a wry mix of clothes, accessories, jewellery and exquisite vintage objects. There are echoes of his Westbourne House HQ, while nodding to Italian tastes. His eclectic vision and high colour is an energising counterpoint to Armani's beige beacon across the street.

☐ TOM FORD
Fashion, Menswear

☎ 02 365 29 600; www.tomford.com; Via Pietro Verri 3; ⏱ 10am-7pm; Ⓜ Montenapoleone

When Tom Ford took over Zegna's old digs he didn't skimp at putting his stamp on the place. A work by current artworld darling Anselm Reyle greets shoppers who are invited to join in a consensual hallucination that they're just visiting a friend's opulently decorated villa. There are actually five floors of madly masculine styling, all for sale. The top floors are reserved for made-to-measure clients, with a bar as well as private bitch'n'stitch lounges.

☐ WANNENES IL XX SECOLO
Antiques

☎ 02 760 22 400; www.wannenes.com; Via Manzoni 16a; ⏱ 11am-5pm Sun, 3.30-7pm Mon, 10am-1pm & 3.30-7pm Tue-Sat; Ⓜ Montenapoleone

Aurelié and Sophie Wannenes father's collecting philosophy was 'a few things but good ones' and it's reflected in their shop of carefully chosen 20th-century furniture, artwork and objects. Among the Deco gems and museum-quality pieces from the likes of Gio Ponti and Fornasetti are unique but affordable treasures.

EAT

ARMANI NOBU
Contemporary Japanese,
Crudo   €€€
☎ 02 623 12 645; www.armaninobu.it;
Via Pisoni 1; ⏱ noon-2.30pm &
7-11.30pm Mon-Sat, 7-11.30pm Sun;
Ⓜ Montenapoleone
A dozen plus years and as many restaurants later, chef Nobuyuki Matsuhisa still mixes continents and cuisines with a certain flair, though one wonders how far the franchise can stretch. You might have seen it all before (and with a lot less hooha), but the Milanese aren't listening. The prices and the people-watching are better in the sultry bar downstairs, where the orange glow turns the overbronzed into Oompa Loompas.

CAFFÉ COVA   *Pasticceria €*
☎ 02 760 05 599; www.pasticceriacova
.com; Via Monte Napoleone ; ⏱ 8.30am-
8pm Mon-Sat; Ⓜ Montenapoleone

It can feel like feeding time at the zoo at Cova's ever crowded bar but the relentlessly charming and attentive baristas won't overlook you, and the surroundings are so soothingly pretty. The sweets case will tempt but a thick-cut smoked salmon on rye is far more fortifying. If you've resisted the temptation to max out your credit card, celebrate with a glass of Cova's own label *prosecco* (sparkling).

DON CARLOS
Contemporary Italian   €€€
☎ 02 723 14 640; www.ristorantedon
carlos.it; Via Alessandro Manzoni 29;
⏱ 7.30-11pm Mon-Sat;
Ⓜ Montenapoleone
Alfredo Russo and Angelo Gangemi will impress the most jaded palate with new combinations (roasted duck leg on potato and cardamom puree with citrus caramel) and reworked classics (steamed artichokes with parmesan mousse and pistachio biscuits) in an old-world postopera setting.

EMPORIO ARMANI CAFFÉ
Contemporary Italian   €€€
☎ 02 723 18 680; Via Crocerossa 2;
⏱ noon-3pm & 8-11pm Mon-Fri,
noon-4pm & 8-11pm Sat, noon-4.30pm
Sun; Ⓜ Montenapoleone
Ne cotton ne' crudo (neither cooked nor raw) is the signature dish at this

Spoil yourself with a glass of bubbly at Caffé Cova

diffusion line cafe in the Armani mothership. It's joined by a simple menu of '70%' organic vegetables, seafood and meat served by male-model waiters. Dine on quiche or club sandwiches or do a long lunch of *bigne di carciofi* (artichoke in choux pastry), followed by beef cheek in aromatic red wine.

IL BARETTO AL BAGLIONI
Italian €€€

☎ 02 781255; Via Senato 5; ⏱ 10-2am; Ⓜ Palestro

When you're feeling a bit bespoke worsted rather than all-new-season-it-bag, trad Baretto does the trick, even if this incarnation

in the Hotel Baglioni is a relatively recent one. The typical Milanese repertoire here includes not only *cotoletta* and osso bucco but the unforgettable *riso salto* (panfried risotto cakes). A not-so-secret door leads from Via della Spiga 6.

IL SALUMAIO DI MONTENAPOLEONE
Italian €€

☎ 02 760 01 123; www.ilsalumaiodimon tenapoleone.it; Via Monte Napoleone 12; ⏱ 11am-7.30pm Mon-Fri; Ⓜ San Babila

Prosecco and *trofie* pesto (Ligurian pasta twists) in an ivy-covered courtyard surrounded by Gucci and Dior: yep, you're in Milan.

Lunch among models trying not to appear terminally bored by their banker boyfriends. The smallgoods and wines in the attached shop are pricey but difficult to pass up.

IL TEATRO Italian €€€

☎ 02 77088; www.fourseasons.com/milan/; Via Gesú 6/8; ⏰ 7.30-11pm Mon-Sat; M Montenapoleone

Service in Il Teatro's lovely but formal dining room within the Four Seasons Hotel is disarmingly, unexpectedly warm and the menu sings with surprisingly smart, unfussy offerings and regional flair. Artisanal products and seasonal ingredients feature and there's a daily tasting menu too.

JOIA Italian, Vegetarian €€€

☎ 02 295 22 124; www.joia.it; Via Panfilo Castaldi 18; ⏰ noon-2.30pm & 7.30pm-midnight Mon-Fri, 7.30pm-midnight Sat; M Porta Venezia; V

Known for seasonal produce and light, clean flavours, the menu at Joia is also imbued with drama and poetry (a winter dish of globe and Jerusalem artichokes, sweet black salsify and pomegranate is entitled 'Beneath a snowy white carpet'). There's the odd overwrought clanger but after one too many servings of leaden

cotoletta, chef Pietro Leeman's green realm is nothing short of delightful. The €40 lunch deal is great value.

PICCOLA ISCHIA Pizzeria €

☎ 02 204 7613; www.piccolaischia.it; Via Giovanni Battista Morgagni 7; ⏰ noon-11pm Mon, Tue, Thu & Fri, 6-11pm Sat & Sun; M Lima

Walls covered in murals of *la bella Napoli* don't always guarantee authenticity, as thousands of suburban pizza joints the world over demonstrate, but once you glimpse the charred, undulating bases, you'll recognise the real thing. The Campanian potato croquettes, *arancini* and zucchini blossoms do nicely for starters. Also at Viale Umbria 60 (p124).

PIZZERIA SPONTINI Pizzeria €€

☎ 02 204 7444; Corso Buenos Aires 60, cnr Via Spontini; ⏰ noon-2pm & 6-11pm Tue-Sun; M Lima

A hot slice isn't a fall back but a first-rate choice at this wood-fired pizza *al trancio* (by the slice) place. The frosted-glass and chrome decor may be new, but traditionalists need have no fear: this is the same dough responsible for rejuvenating Corso Buenos Aires shoppers since 1953.

TRATTORIA DI GIANNINO *Italian* €€€
☎ 02 669 86 998; www.ristorante
giannino.it; Via Vittor Pisani 6;
🕙 noon-3pm & 6pm-12.30am;
Ⓜ Repubblica

Dark wood chairs against a
subdued palette of white and
brick red walls makes for an
endearingly posh dining room.
Serves are large and there are
absolutely no surprises on the
menu (osso bucco, *cotoletta*, warm
seafood salad), and that's why
everyone likes it.

WARSA *Eritrean* €€
☎ 02 201673; www.ristorantewarsa.it;
Via Melzo 16; 🕙 closed Wed;
Ⓜ Porta Venezia

Warm, elegant and atmospheric,
Warsa serves authentic curries –
lentil, beef or fish – Eritrean-style
atop *injera* (flat bread). Eating is
done with your hands. There's
also a selection of South
African wine.

🍸 DRINK
🍸 BAR BASSO *Bar*
☎ 02 294 00 580; www.barbasso.com;
Via Plinio 39; 🕙 7-1am Wed-Mon;
Ⓜ Lima

Historic home of the *sbagliato*
(the Negroni made with *prosecco*
instead of gin), as well as the
brilliant concept of *mangia e*
bevi (eat and drink), involving a
supersized goblet of strawberries,
zabaglione, chocolate and a large
slug of some kind of booze. Don't
try it at home.

🍸 DIANA GARDEN *Bar*
☎ 02 205 82 081; Viale Piave 42;
🕙 10-1am; Ⓜ Porta Venezia

Seasonally updated to keep
you guessing, the bar is secreted
by a vast leather curtain at the
back of the Sheraton Diana's
lobby. Grab a freshly crushed
peach Bellini and lounge beside
the magnificent windows –
the perfect possie to see who's
making a tit of themselves in
the lush, low-lit garden. The
aperitivo buffet is one of the city's
most rich and varied, though with
drinks nudging €15 you'd
be hoping for more
than bruschetta.

🍸 JUST CAVALLI CAFÉ *Bar*
☎ 02 311 8171; www.justcavallicafe.com;
Via della Spiga 30; 🕙 8pm-2am;
Ⓜ Montenapoleone

Roberto Cavalli has never been
one for subtlety, and, from the
lift trip downwards, his basement
cafe is no exception. Part padded-
cell, part octopuses garden, it's
best to grab a brightly coloured
cocktail and go with it.

L'ELEPHANTE *Bar*
☎ 02 295 18 768; Via Melzo 22;
⏱ 7pm-2am; Ⓜ Porta Venezia
The expert bartender here is happiest when mixing things up and the same can be said of the alternative-trendy crowd, which tends towards lesbian-and-gay-friendly or the generically open-minded. The setting is equally eclectic: no two chairs are the same and the snack buffet is diverse.

LINO'S COFFEE *Cafe*
☎ 02 763 17 925; www.linoscoffee.com; Corso Venezia 37; ⏱ 7am-7pm; Ⓜ Palestro
While Italy never needed an answer to Starbucks, Parma-import Lino's takes up the challenge nicely with highly credible coffee and some oddly appealing variations on a theme. 'Coffee Crack', for one. The locals love it, in case you were wondering.

MARTINI BAR *Bar*
☎ 02 760 11 154;
www.dolcegabbana.it; Corso Venezia 15;
⏱ 10am-10pm Mon-Sat;
Ⓜ San Babila
Seen through the bottom of a martini glass, the glossy black marble walls, jellyfishlike Murano chandelier and neon signage can bring on '80s flashbacks, even if you weren't there first time around.

⭐ PLAY

ARMANI PRIVÉ *Club*
☎ 02 623 12 655; Via Gastone Pisoni, cnr Via Manzoni 31;
⏱ 10.30pm-3am Tue-Sat;
Ⓜ Montenapoleone
In the basement of the Armani superstore, this club has a subtle Japanese-Modernist aesthetic, the calm of which you'll need after the hysteria of getting in and clocking the drink prices. Boobs, botox and blonde hair (or a dinner booking at Nobu) will help with the door police.

DOLCE & GABBANA BEAUTY FARM *Spa*
☎ 02 760 01 348; Corso Venezia 15;
⏱ 2-7pm Mon, 10am-9pm Tue & Fri, 10am-7pm Wed, Thu & Sat;
Ⓜ San Babila
Spend a day on the Beauty Farm, and emerge scrubbed, massaged, mani-pedicured and fresh-faced. Treatments take place in a campy clinical setting that screams 'trust me, I'm an aesthetician'. There's also a wittily retro men's barber.

E'SPA AT GIANFRANCO FERRÉ *Spa*

☎ 02 760 17 526; www.gianfrancoferre
.com; Via Sant'Andrea 15; ⏱ 10am-
10pm Tue-Fri, 10am-9pm Sat, 11am-8pm
Sun; Ⓜ San Babila

Luxurious surrounds – waxed
stucco and shiny wood walls, a
Bisazza glass-mosaic floor in black
and gold, a private garden – aim
for 'refound sensuousness'. Forget
about wrinkles and detox, just
enjoy the moment: chromatherapy
lights turn your shower into a
liquid rainbow, and subtle aromatic
oils pervade the air.

SPA GUERLAIN AT HOTEL BAGLIONI *Spa*

☎ 02 454 73 111; www.baglionihotels
.com; Via Senato 5; ⏱ 9am-9pm Mon-
Sat, 10am-6pm Sun; Ⓜ Montenapoleone

A spot of 'body sublimation' at
this white but warm spa isn't as
against instinct as the name might
suggest. Treatments range from
the reassuringly conventional
to the gently holistic, with
hydrotherapy, Vichy showers
and footbaths working their
watery wonders.

>BRERA

Just northwest of La Scala is the neighbourhood of Brera. Its tight cobbled streets and ancient buildings are an instant reminder that Milan was not always a modern metropolis. Not so long ago, it was a study in boho raffishness. While there's still plenty of galleries, artisan's workshops and gaggles of dreadlocked art students, they are quickly being outnumbered by hairdressers, designer stationery shops and chichi bars. That's not to say it's not a delightful spot for gallery hopping, shopping, drinks or dinner; Vie Vetero and Mercato have some of Milan's best options for each. Behind high walls at the neighbourhood's heart is the 17th-century Palazzo di Brera, originally a Jesuit college, though occupied by the Accademia di Belle Arti since 1776. The art school has trained some of Milan's most interesting people, including artist Lucio Fontana, Nobel Laureate playwright Dario Fo and designer Piero Fornasetti. Past the Canova statue of Napoleon and the stairs is the Pinacoteca di Brera, Milan's famous painting collection. To the north, the area merges seamlessly into the nightlife area of Corso Como.

BRERA

◉ SEE
Galleria Francesca
 Kaufmann 1 B7
Orto Botanico 2 D6
Pinacoteca di Brera 3 C5

▣ SHOP
Antonia Boutique 4 B7
Atribu 5 A4
Cavalli e Nastri 6 C7
Crazy Art 7 B6
Edra 8 C7
Fabriano 9 B7
Galante Visconti 10 C5

Kristina Ti 11 C4
La Vertrina di Beryl 12 C3
Mr N............................. 13 C7
Olfattorio Bar à
 Parfums 14 C5
Rigadritto 15 C7
TAD 16 B3
Viativoli 17 B7
Zeiss 18 B7

⑪ EAT
Fioraio Bianchi Caffé 19 D3
Latteria 20 C3
Lo's Chinese Takeaway .. 21 B6
Obika 22 B6

Pescheria da Claudio 23 B7
Pizzeria Grand'Italia..... 24 B4

▾ DRINK
Art Café 25 C5
Bar Jamaica 26 C5
Bulgari Hotel 27 D6
N'ombra de vin 28 C5

▥ PLAY
Bulgari Spa ....(see 27)
Piccolo Teatro Strehler 29 A5

Please see over for map

◎ SEE

◎ GALLERIA FRANCESCA KAUFMANN

☎ 02 720 94 331; www.francescakauf
mann.com; Via dell'Orso 16; ☺ 11am-
7.30pm Tue-Fri, 2-7.30pm Sat;
🚇 1 to Ponte Vetero

Good for site-specific, ambitiously
conceptual work. Kaufmann shows
a number of young Milan-based
artists, including Gianni Caravaggio
(no relation), Adrian Paci, Maggie
Cardelus and Pier Paolo Campanini.

◎ ORTO BOTANICO

Via Brera 28, entry through Accademia di
Brera; ☺ 9am-noon & 1-4pm Mon-Fri;
🚇 Lanza

Maria Teresa had the towering
gingko planted here in 1777,
when she turned the former Jesuit
veggie patch into an open air lec-
ture hall for budding botanists
(the wunderkind of the Enlight-
enment). This fragrant, walled
garden is still filled with medicinal
plants and is a perfect nature fix
after the culture onslaught of
the Pinacoteca.

◎ PINACOTECA DI BRERA

☎ 02 722631; www.brera.beniculturali
.it; Via Brera 28; admission €5/2.50;
☺ 8.30am-7.15pm Tue-Sun; 🚇 Lanza

Religious art amassed (or rather,
purloined) by Napoleon formed
the basis of the formidable

Gaze at the amazing works of art at Pinacoteca di Brera

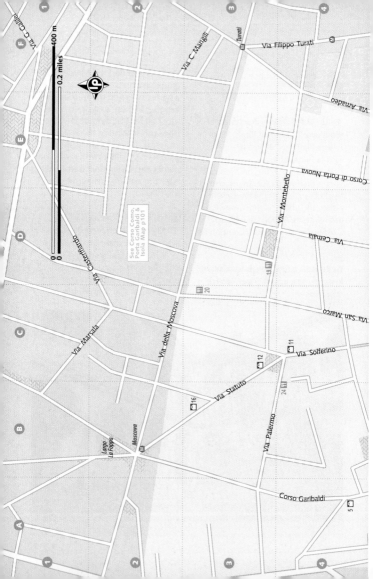

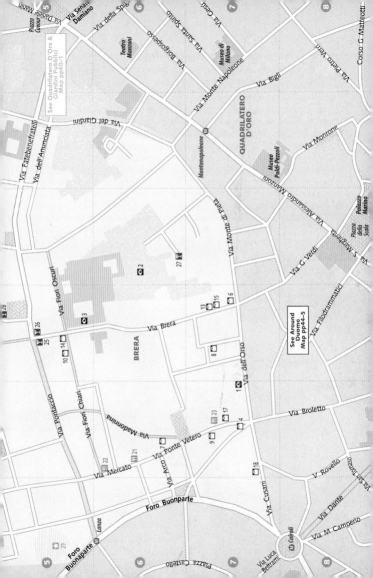

Chiara Agnello & Roberta Tenconi
Curators, Careof & Fondazione Trussardi

Where to for contemporary art? Incredibly Milan still lacks a dedicated museum of contemporary art but it's always had an entrepreneurial culture and dynamic private initiatives. Milan hosts the most important Italian private foundations: Hangar Bicocca, Prada and Nicola Trussardi, plus many commercial galleries. **What about emerging artists?** That's harder; Careof/ViaFarini or look for *Brown Magazine* (www.brownmagazine.it) and *Mousse Magazine* (www.moussemagazine.it). **Who's hot right now?** *Flash Art* magazine has tried to define them…but the list is too long! **Must-sees?** Casa Boschi di Stefano, for Fontana, Manzoni, Morandi and the Italian Informel painters of the 1950s; Studio Castiglioni; the Dan Flavin installation at Chiesa Rossa; the view from the top of Duomo Cathedral or Torre Branca; Colonne di San Lorenzo with an aperitif; jazz at Blue Note. **Art crowd aperitivo favourites?** La Triennale, Bar Basso, Frida, La Belle Aurore, Pane e Acqua, Birrificio di Lambrate.

collection housed at the upstairs galleries of the Palazzo di Brera. On show here are pieces by Raphael, both Bellinis, Rembrandt, Mantegna, della Francesca and Caravaggio (see p17).

SHOP

ANTONIA BOUTIQUE
Fashion, Accessories

☎ 02 869 98 340; www.antonia.it; Via Ponte Vetero 1; 🕑 3-7pm Mon, 10am-7pm Tue-Sat; 🚇 1 Ⓜ Lanza

New-breed buyer Antonia Giancinti's eponymous boutique mixes locals like Bottega Veneta with international labels like Lam, Lavin, Biba and McCartney in an urban, monochrome space that echoes her Carrie Bradshaw-ish aesthetic. **Antonia Accessori** (☎ 02 869 0216; Via Cusani 4; 🕑 3-7pm Mon, 10am-7pm Tue-Sat; 🚇 1 Ⓜ Lanza) displays the same brash zeitgeistiness. Trust her, she's a self-proclaimed shoe-victim (and she's not talking bunions).

ATRIBU *Fashion*
☎ 02 867127; Corso Garibaldi 49; 🕑 3.30-7.30pm Mon, 10.30am-7.30pm Tue-Sat; Ⓜ Lanza

If brands that advertise on billboards are not your thing, Atribu features a host of young Italian designers (including the Japan-based Rossella Carrara), interest-ing labels from Sweden, Belgium and Japan and the odd one-off treasure.

CAVALLI E NASTRI
Vintage fashion

☎ 02 720 00 449; www.cavallienastri .com; Via Brera 2; 🕑 10am-7pm; 🚇 Ponte Vetero

The Milanese took a while to take to vintage (Won't people think I'm poor? How will anyone know what label it is?), but this gorgeously colourful shop in the heart of Brera has led the way. Stock is mostly sourced from mythical early and mid 20th-century Italian fashion houses, lovingly curated and priced accordingly (some mediocre '70s pieces rather cheekily so).

CRAZY ART *Antiques*
☎ 02 875212; www.crazyart-milano.com; Via Madonnina 11; 🕑 9.30am-12.30pm & 2.30-6pm Mon-Fri; Ⓜ Lanza

When you really must have a boar skeleton, Victorian kiosk, a few de-mented rocking horses or a ship's steering wheel. Leave the real world at the door. Did someone just say fashion shoot?

EDRA *Furniture, Design*
☎ 02 869 95 122; www.edra.com; Via Ciovassino 3; 🕑 10.30am-7.30pm Tue-Sat; 🚇 1 Ⓜ Lanza

Masanori Umeda's Gothic rose chair looks like it will eat you up whole if you dare to take your feet off the floor, and the Campana brother's Leatherworks one seems as if salvaged from the *Beyond Thunderdome* props lot. During its 20-year history, Edra has never played safe and the Italian swagger and sauciness of its products can be an acquired taste, but one that promises a lot of fun.

☐ FABRIANO
Stationery, Accessories

02 763 18 754; www.fabrianoboutique
.com; Via Ponte Vetero 17; ☼ 1-7.30pm
Mon, 10am-7.30pm Tue-Sat; ⓧ 1
Ⓜ Lanza

Stationery-tragics won't be the only ones going quietly ga-ga over Fabriano's goods. Everything from plain notebooks to linen pencil cases to kooky leather keyrings are exquisitely crafted. An ever-present sense of wit makes all the good taste even more attractive. Staff are delightful and wrap gifts with trademark flair.

☐ GALANTE VISCONTI
Jewellery

☎ 02 869 98 876; www.galantevisconti
.com; Via Fiori Chiari 2; ☼ 11am-
7.30pm; Ⓜ Lanza

The handmade creations here are undeniably luxe but have an earthy, rock-and-roll edge. Rough beaten pink gold surrounds deep pink tourmalines in delicate,

ancient-looking earrings, diamond-clad circles swivel on rings evoking the innards of preindustrial machinery.

☐ KRISTINA TI *Fashion*

☎ 02 653379; www.kristinati.com; Via Solferino 18; ☼ 10am-7pm; Ⓜ Moscova

Kristina Ti specialises in the swooningly pretty, but never one-dimensionally girly. Slips and lingerie can be nicely boxed as gifts.

☐ LA VETRINA DI BERYL *Shoes*

☎ 02 654278; Via Statuto 4;
☼ 10am-7pm Mon-Sat; Ⓜ Moscova

Barbara Beryl's name was known to cultists around the world, way before Manolo became a byword for female desire. Stumbling upon this deceptively nondescript shop is like chancing upon the shoe-racks at a *Vogue Italia* photo shoot. Edgier pieces from Prada, Marc Jacobs and Costume National are joined by practically certifiable eccentrics like Paul Harden. There's a rack or two of clothes too.

☐ MR N
Homewares, Accessories

☎ 02 720 93 420; www.misterenne.it;
Via Brera 8; ☼ 10.30am-7.30pm Tue-Sat,
3.30-7.30pm Sun & Mon; ⓧ Ponte Vetero

Maurizia Dova's brightly striped and flower-strewn textiles, both in plain cotton and pvc-coated oil-cloth versions, can be had by the metre right off the roll, or come

MILAN'S MOVING TRICOLORE: RED, YELLOW & GREEN

In 1958, Gianni Roghi, eagerly anticipating the building of a subway, wrote 'The most hurried people on the peninsula…live in a city which, at least four times a day, is condemned to slowness'. Milan's Metropolitana Milanese (metro for short) is a product of the city's second economic boom of the '50s and '60s and was seen as a gesture of civic patriotism as much as a way to solve traffic jams. Its first line, the red or M1, was opened in 1964, and was joined by the green line (M2) in 1969. Stations and branches were added through the '60s and '70s, and the yellow line (M3) completed in 1990.

Architect Franco Albini designed the M1 and M2, with a team that included Antonio Piva, Albini's wife Franca Helg and Bob Noorda, the latter two responsible for the innovative graphics and signature 'M'. The designers' use of colour coding and simple functional materials has been incredibly influential, becoming an international design icon. In fact, Amendola and Caiazzo stations are deemed national treasures, as they remain relatively untouched. Cadorna and San Babila also demonstrate the same modernist vision, despite extensive renovations.

The system is still a work in progress, with more planned extensions and new lines – light blue, purple and orange (M4, 5 & 6) – hopefully ready for Expo2015.

beautifully made up into wallets, pouches and luggage. Illustration-adorned handbags, cheekily-inscribed knickers and Sandrine Fabre's sweet tin boxes are also to be found in this imaginative shop.

◫ OLFATTORIO BAR À PARFUMS *Perfume*
☎ 02 720 04 400; Via Brera 23;
🕑 11am-2.30pm & 3-7.30pm Tue-Sat;
Ⓜ Lanza

This huge shop sells a wide range of perfumes including L'Artisan Perfumier, Les Parfums de Rosine, Dyptyque and La Compagnie de Provence. While the selection is broad, it's not particularly cutting edge, but the woody salonlike decor makes for lovely back of wrist sniffing.

◫ RIGADRITTO
Gifts, Homewares
☎ 02 805 82 936; Via Brera 6;
🕑 10.30am-7.30pm; 🚊 Ponte Vetero

Loads of little stickers, clips, pencils and decorated stationery fill this graphic, colourful space. Cat and dog T-shirts that turn humans into pets are delightful.

◫ TAD *Fashion*
☎ 02 655 06 731; www.taditaly.com;
Via Statuto 12; 🕑 10.30am-7.30pm
Tue-Sat, noon-8pm Sun; Ⓜ Moscova

This 'concept store' could have done with a few less of those concept thingies; its mishmash of styles is so desperate to please it's hard to get to the Proenza Schuler, Balenciaga and Hussein Chalayan without wanting to slap someone.

NEIGHBOURHOODS

BRERA

If you can grin and bare it, there's also a hairdresser, homewares department and cafe.

🛒 VIATIVOLI *Fashion*
☎ 02 867997; Via Ponte Vetero 6;
🕒 10.30am-7.30pm Mon-Sat;
Ⓜ Lanza or Carioli or tram

Well-cut trousers might be a prosaic claim to fame, but this Milanese stalwart's simple suiting for women comes with enough interesting twists to keep customers faithful. Any hint of stuffiness is dispelled with stripy tees and mix-and-match bikini separates in smartly white-sprigged navy and red.

🛒 ZEISS *Shoes*
☎ 02 869 15 563; Via Cusani 10;
🕒 10am-7pm Tue-Sun; 🚃 1 Ⓜ Lanza

Milan's miles of cobblestones and days of drizzle can make the most dedicated heel-wearer weep. Take a cue from locals who don Bikkemberg trainers for day. Patent and metallic options are available for those who refuse to entirely discard glam. There's also a large range for children and men.

🍽 EAT
🍽 FIORAIO BIANCHI CAFFÈ
Italian, French   €€
☎ 02 290 14 390; www.fioraiobianchi caffe.it; Via Montebello 7; 🕒 8am-midnight Mon-Sat; Ⓜ Moscova

RAW LIKE SUSHI

As anyone who's been to the Puglian coast will know, Italians love their *crudo*, raw seafood, as much as the Japanese. They are also fond of *carpaccio*, paper-thin raw beef or horse. *Crudo's* appeal draws on the same taste and texture elements as sushi – a deceptively simple balance of fat, salt, acid – but uses olive oil, vinegar or citrus, seasalt and pepper instead of soy, pickle and wasabi. The Milanese can't get enough, either Italian-style, trad Japanese or a fusion of the two, and strangely often refer to all forms of *crudo* as 'sushi'. For fabulously fresh and simple fish, try Da Claudio (p86), for a deluxe Milanese-Japanese fusion twist head to Zéro (p149) or do smart sushi and sashimi at Maru (p124) or Iyo (p95).

This former florist's shop is great for a subtly French lunch, or an excellent *aperitivo* among the flowers. Dinners are fresh and inventive with particularly delicious border-crossing desserts, from Provencal lavender brulee to an Arab-inflected cassata cup. The decor either delights (ooh! glasses inscribed with *amour* and *bonheur*!) or reminds you of someone you don't like.

🍽 LATTERIA *Italian*   €€
☎ 02 659 7653; Via San Marco 24;
🕒 12.30-2.30pm & 7.30-10pm Mon-Fri;
Ⓜ Moscova

If you can snare a seat in this tiny and ever-popular restaurant, you'll find dishes like fusilli with herbed ricotta and spring onions, a faro (spelt) salad with buffalo mozzarella and tomato or *riso al salto* (risotto fritters) among the ever-changing, mostly organic, menu.

LO'S CHINESE TAKEAWAY
Chinese €

☎ 02 864 60 944; Via Mercato 14;
🕑 11am-2pm daily, 5-10pm Tue-Sun;
Ⓜ Lanza

Crowded with locals from Milan's Chinese community, this is an ultracheap alternative to heading up to Chinatown. It's a standard *Cinese*-style menu but they don't spare the spice and portions are generous.

OBIKA
Italian, Mozzarella bar €€

☎ 02 864 50 568; www.obika.it;
Via Mercato, cnr Via Fiori Chiari;
🕑 noon-3.30pm & 6-11pm Mon-Sat, set Italian brunch noon-3pm & 6-11pm Sun;
Ⓜ Lanza

Milan's main branch of the Obika empire is stylish, with glass-box displays and French army chairs. Ordering is simple. Take your pick of *mozzarella di bufala* (buffalo-milk mozzarella balls), from sweet to smoked, then choose an accompaniment (ranging from salads to prosciutto). The €8 *aperitivo* here is a shockingly good deal, an all-you-can-eat array of *bufala*-strewn salads, cold meats, salmon and simple, delicious pastas, and a *sbagliato* (a sparkling wine, Antico Rosso and Campari cocktail).

Help yourself to the all-you-can-eat spread at Obika

🍴 PESCHERIA DA CLAUDIO
Crudo €€

☎ 02 805 6857; www.pescheriadaclaudio.it; Via Ponte Vetero 16; ⏰ 8.30am-2.30pm & 4-9pm Tue-Sat; Ⓜ Lanza 🚊 3, 4

Join the savvy suits for a power lunch or early dinner of *pesce crudo* (raw fish). Plates loaded with marinated tuna, mixed salmon, tuna and white fish with pistachios or lightly blanched octopus 'carpaccio' are consumed standing along bars facing the fishmonger's produce, with a glass of light fizz.

🍴 PIZZERIA GRAND'ITALIA
Pizzeria €

☎ 02 877759; Via Palermo 5; ⏰ noon-3pm & 7pm-1am; Ⓜ Moscova

Favoured by bar-hopping *ragazzi* as well as families, this Brera institution serves traditional Milanese-style pizza *a trancio* (by the slab). Paper-thin pizza may be in elsewhere, but thick's the way they like it round here.

🍸 DRINK

🍸 ART CAFÉ *Bar*

☎ 02 805 3612; www.artcafebrera.com; Via Brera 23; ⏰ 8-2am Mon-Fri, 9-2.30am Sat & Sun; Ⓜ Lanza

Along with Bar Jamaica across the way, Art Café's tables take over this pedestrianised part of Via Brera making for a lively street scene. There's a certain relief in Art Café's recalcitrant lack of style, though it can't quite do authentic grunge either. But there's free wi-fi, cheap *aperitivo* and a blessed lack of attitude.

🍸 BAR JAMAICA *Bar*

☎ 02 876723; www.jamaicabar.it; Via Brera 32; ⏰ 8-2am Mon-Sat, 8am-8.30pm Sun; Ⓜ Lanza

Bar Jamaica may no longer be the Bohemian dive that gave Milan a fleeting reputation for brains as well as style, but it's still an unpretentious watering hole. Students from nearby Accademia di Brera nurse drinks for days on coveted sidewalk seats.

🍸 BULGARI HOTEL *Bar*

☎ 02 805 8051; www.bulgarihotel.com; Via Privata Fratelli Gabba 7/b; ⏰ 7.30-1am; Ⓜ Montenapoleone

Whether it's inside beneath the giant botanical sculptures at the earth-toned bar or outside on the terrace overlooking the brilliantly green garden, the *aperitivo* scene here is an intense slice of Milan life. The second-cheapest wine on the list may weigh in at €20 but it's cheap for the theatre, darling. The restaurant serves a refreshingly light Med menu, and an al-fresco summer lunch is a treat.

🍸 N'OMBRA DE VIN *Enoteca*

☎ 02 659 9650; www.nombradevin.it; Via San Marco 2; ⏰ 9am-midnight Mon-Sat; Ⓜ Moscova

BEEN THERE, DRANK THAT: LOMBARD WINES

Franciacorta DOCG The breakout star of Lombard wines, this sparkling white is a relative newcomer developed in the 1950s using the French *methode champenoise*. No upscale Milanese menu could do without it, and it's got a DOCG quality denomination (a cut above DOC).

Lugana DOC Fine seafood demands something extra, and this underappreciated charmer from Lombardy's border with the Veneto shows crisp flair.

Lambrusco Mantovano DOC Rules were made to be broken, and this light-hearted and slightly fizzy (yes, fizzy) red has been a Milanese favourite for more than a millennium.

Oltrepó Pavese Barbera DOC Riots broke out in the Middle Ages when Milan was cut off from Oltrepó, Lombardy's most renowned wine region. You'll relate when you sip this rousing Barbera, a must with rich dishes like osso bucco.

Valtellina DOCG Like a well-behaved Milanese dinner companion, this red is dry, distinctive and rich without being too forward – da Vinci loved the stuff.

This *enoteca* is set in a former Augustine refectory, and it retains a Catholic approach to wine. Tastings can be had all day and bottles start at reasonable prices. There's also a small bistro if all that swilling sees you work up an appetite. Risotto Milanese is topped with artichoke and breadcrumbs, white asparagus is served with quail eggs, and a tartar of Piedmontese beef is enriched with aged balsamic.

PLAY

BULGARI SPA *Spa*

☎ 02 805 8051; www.bulgarihotel.com; **Via Privata Fratelli Gabba 7/b;** ⏰ **facilities 7.30am-11.30pm, appointments 9am-10pm;** Ⓜ **Montenapoleone**
This warm, enveloping space in the basement of the Antonio Cittero–designed hotel instils immediate calm. Espa aromatherapy treatments target pressure points and chakras; whether you're a believer or not, there's no doubt they will relax and rejuvenate a frazzled traveller. Make sure to amortise the sky-high prices with a dip in the gorgeous gold-mosaic lined pool or a lounge in the ethereal steam room.

PICCOLO TEATRO STREHLER *Theatre*

☎ 02 424 11 889; www.piccoloteatro .org; Largo Greppi; ⏰ box office 10am-6.45pm Mon-Sat, 1-6.30pm Sun; Ⓜ Lanza
This Marco Zanuso–designed theatre was opened more than 10 years ago to address the size restraints of the original and has gone on to become one of Milan's cultural powerhouses. The large complex includes the Teatro Studio at Via Rivoli, 6.

>PARCO SEMPIONE

Castello Sforzesco's dark imposing battlements sit at the end of Via Dante. Walk through the grand central passageway to one of its many museums, or en route to Parco Sempione, and modern Milan slips away. The park beyond is a leafy oasis with ponds, winding paths and a lush fairway of iridescent grass that on sunny Sundays attracts footballers and drummers alike. Nestled on the southwestern edge are design museum Design Triennale and Gio Ponti's Meccano-esque Torre Branca. To the northwest, the Arco della Pace heralds the road to Paris, as well as a cluster of pumping bars. The wide Corso Sempione is lined with elegant apartment buildings; to its south is the RAI HQ and the old Fiera Milano exhibition complex, set to be reborn as CityLife. Northwest, the neighbourhood is well-to-do but not flashy, and boasts another bar strip tucked away in Via Piero della Francesca. Northeast is Milan's Chinatown, itself well on the road to gentrification, and the melancholy expanses of the Cimitero Monumentale. You'll find one of Milan's densest collections of street art nestled between the two at the end of Via Donato Bramante.

PARCO SEMPIONE

👁 SEE

Careof, Docva & Viafarini	1	F2
Castello Sforzesco	2	G6
Cimitero Monumentale	3	F1
Civico Aquario	4	G4
Parco Sempione	5	F5
Studio Museo Achille Castiglioni	6	F6
Torre Branca	7	E5
Triennale di Milano	8	E5

🛍 SHOP

Art Book Triennale	9	F5
Officina Slowear	10	F4

🍴 EAT

Chatulle	11	C1
Iyo	12	C1
Jubin	13	F2
La Cantina di Manuela	14	E2
La Cantina di Via Mussi	15	D2
L'Altra Pharmacia	16	F3
Lyr	17	D2
Sergio & Efisio	18	D3
Trattoria degli Orti	19	D2
Triennale Design Café	20	E5

🍸 DRINK

Bar Bianco	21	F5
Bhangra Bar	22	E4

Cantine Isola	23	F3
Just Cavalli Café	24	E5
Living	25	E4
Milano	26	E2
Old Fashion Café	27	E5
Roialto	28	C1
Siddharta Buddha Cafe	29	F4
Stalingrado	30	C1
Wagamaga	31	D2

⭐ PLAY

Gattopardo	32	C2

Please see over for map

SEE

CAREOF, DOCVA & VIAFARINI

☎ 02 331 5800; www.docva.org; Fabbrica del Vapore, Via Giulio Cesare Procaccini 4; ⏱ 3-7pm Tue-Sat; 🚋 29, 30, 33
This contemporary art complex is home to three long-running nonprofit organisations. Careof and Viafarini are on the ground floor and show the work of emerging artists, often installation-based or using new technologies. On the 1st floor, Docva (Documentation Center for Visual Arts) holds an extensive archive of books, magazines, videos and artists' portfolios (access by appointment only).

CASTELLO SFORZESCO

☎ 02 884 63 700; www.milanocastello.it; Piazza Castello; admission €3/1.50, after 2pm Fri free; ⏱ castle grounds 7am-7pm, museums 9am-5.30pm Tue-Sun; Ⓜ Cairoli
Originally a Visconti fortress, this immense red-brick castle was later home to the mighty Sforza dynasty that ruled Renaissance Milan. The castle's defences were designed by the multitalented da Vinci; Napoleon later drained the moat and removed the drawbridges. Today it shelters 10 specialised museums (one ticket allows entry to all). Among the standouts are the **Museo d'Arte Antica**, containing Michelangelo's last, unfinished

Stroll through beautiful Parco Sempione (p92)

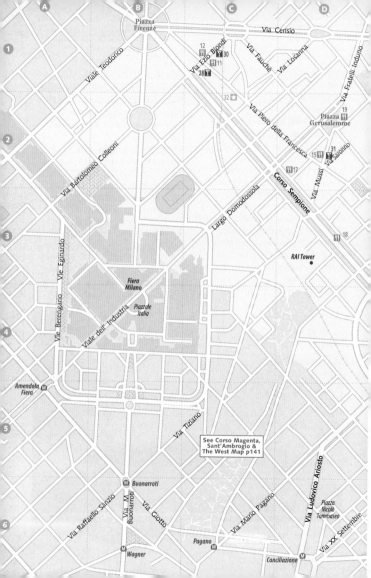

work, *Pietà Rondanini*; paintings by Bellini, Tiepolo, Mantegna, Titian and van Dyck in the **Pinacoteca e Raccolte d'Arte**; local archaeological finds at the **Museo della Preistoria**; and early musical instruments in the **Museo degli Strumenti Musicali**.

☏ CIMITERO MONUMENTALE
☎ **02 884 65 600;** ⌚ **8am-6pm Tue-Sun;** Ⓜ **Garibaldi**

Behind striking Renaissance-revival black-and-white walls, Milan's wealthy have kept their dynastic ambitions alive long after death with grand sculptural gestures since 1866. Nineteenth-century death-the-maiden eroticism gives way to some fabulous abstract forms from midcentury masters. Studio BBPR's geometric steel-and-marble memorial to Milan's WWII concentration camp dead is stark and moving. Grab a map inside the forecourt – it's easy to get lost.

☏ CIVICO ACQUARIO
☎ **02 864 62 051; Viale Gadio 2; www.verdeacqua.eu;** ⌚ **9am-1pm & 2-5.30pm Tue-Sun;** Ⓜ **Lanza**

You'll be transfixed by the aquatic art nouveau facade, but kids will race ahead to see Lombardy's fish on display at Europe's third-oldest aquarium. Turns out mountain streams make for rather predictable silver on silver fish, but that

only makes the red anemones more splashy and the balletic boarfish real prima donnas.

☏ PARCO SEMPIONE
⌚ **6.30am-nightfall;** Ⓜ **Cadorna**

Everything you'd expect from Milan is here: a historic castle (Castello Sforzesco), chic bars, a museum honouring design (Triennale di Milano), lovely Liberty-style buildings (Civico Acquario) and an architectural conversation piece (Torre Branca). Plus there's grass, winding paths, relaxed people, and peace and quiet, too.

☏ STUDIO MUSEO ACHILLE CASTIGLIONI
☎ **02 724 34 231; Piazza Castello 27 (ring the buzzer marked Studio Castiglioni); tours free with prepurchased Triennale di Milan ticket (€8/6; see p94);** ⌚ **10am, 11am & noon Tue-Sun (bookings required);** Ⓜ **Cadorna**

Architect, designer and teacher Achille Castiglioni was one of Italy's most influential 20th-century thinkers. This is the studio where he worked daily until his death in 2002, and the hour-long tours vividly illuminate his intelligent but playful creative process. Details abound; job folders printed with specially produced numerical stamps reach to the ceiling, scale models of his Hilly sofa for Cassina decorate a drawing table and a host of inspirational objects from

Gionvanna Castiglioni
Studio Museo Achille Castiglioni

The mission? To show how Achille worked, projected and lived in his studio. Also to archive his technical drawings, sketches, prototypes, photographs, slides, books, magazines and objects. **Achilles' greatest legacy?** The idea of a free way of life: useful and essential, without frill or overdoing. **Your father's design you love most?** An electric switch that was an 'unsigned' project from 1968 – it's still used by electricians today and costs €1. It makes a very nice click-clack sound! **Where to find 'living design'?** Flos, Zanotta, Alessi, De Padova and Danese continue to produce and/or sell objects designed by Achille and others of his milieu. **Favourite corner of the city?** The Natural History Museum in the wonderful Giardini Pubblici (p63), and the Liberty buildings in nearby Via Serbelloni (go and admire the sculpture by Adolfo Wildt: a big ear in marble that acted as an intercom).

ART OUTPOST

Once Milan's industrial powerhouse, the neighbourhood of Bovisa is being transformed into a hub for research, science and technology, centred on the Politecnico di Milano. **Triennale Bovisa** (☎ 02 657 7801; www.triennalebovisa.it; Via Lambruschini 31; ⏰ 11am-11pm Tue-Sun; 🚊 Villapizone, Bovisa) is a temporary contemporary art space that during its four-year existence plays host to a programme of exhibitions, events and cinema. Milan's street artists have been invited to sign the wall of the surrounding area, also creating a living gallery of graffiti and stencil work. There is also a beautifully designed onsite bistro open from 10am to 2am Tuesday to Saturday.

joke glasses to bicycle seats await discovery.

🎯 TORRE BRANCA

☎ 02 331 4120; Via Camoens, Parco Sempione; lift ticket €3; ⏰ 10.30am-2pm, 2.30-7pm & 9.30pm-midnight Tue-Sun; Ⓜ Cadorna

The spindly legs on this steel tower may not inspire you to take the 10-minute lift ride 108m to the viewing platform, but not to worry: Gió Ponti's 1930s engineering feat was safety-reinforced as recently as 2003. Go at night to watch city lights twinkle, and lord it over the Just Cavalli Café crowd below. Opening hours vary seasonally; call to confirm.

🎯 TRIENNALE DI MILANO

☎ 02 724 34 212; www.triennaledesign museum.it; Viale Emilio Alemanga 6; admission €8/6; ⏰ 10.30am-8.30pm Tue-Sun; Ⓜ Cadorna

Regular shows in the Triennale building have championed design practice since its inception in the

1930s, but its permanent museum dedicated to Italian design was only launched late in 2007. Across a symbolic bridge, the inaugural survey of iconic objects and furniture (including Pesce's supersized Moloch lamp, Sottsass' Memphis pieces and outdoor Kartell and Cassina stools in situ on the roof) is organised around seven principles that traverse Latin animism, the upright Milanese middle-class and Futurist dynamism. Peter Greenaway and crew's projections only serve to highlight some rather flimsy propositions; in any case, the work speaks for itself.

🛍 SHOP

📕 ART BOOK TRIENNALE
Bookshop

☎ 02 890 13 403; www.artbooktriennale .com; Viale Emilio Alemagna 6; ⏰ 10.30am-8.30pm Tue-Sun; Ⓜ Cadorna

Run by Lambrate's fabulous Art Book outfit (p104), this shop is as enthralling as the exhibitions themselves. There's a full range of beautifully produced catalogues as well as titles from Electa, Rizzoli, Thames & Hudson, Phaidon and MIT Press, and design piece children's books from Corraini.

OFFICINA SLOWEAR *Fashion*
☎ 02 331 00 774; www.slowear.com; **Viale Elvezia 6;** ✆ 10am-7pm Mon-Sat; M Moscova

Slowear takes its cue from the Slow Food philosophy and markets a stable of labels (Incotex, Zanone) that all fit a wearable, reasonably timeless and beautifully tactile bill. Perfect for scouting a new office wardrobe.

EAT
CHATULLE *Italian*   €€
☎ 02 345 34 024; www.chatulle.it; **Via Piero della Francesca 68;** ✆ noon-3pm & 7pm-3am; ⛟ 1,14,19, 33

The white on white thing here is so relentless, you might think you've ended up at one of Puffy's summer dos, or in the Queen of Narnia's palace. The food, although served on very large, see-through plates, is surprisingly straightforward, classic Italian (in all its many hues). Staff are welcoming; patrons dress to match the surrounds.

IYO *Japanese*   €€€
☎ 02 454 76 898; www.iyo.it; **Via Piero della Francesca 74;** ✆ noon-2.45pm & 7.30-11.45pm Tue-Sun; ⛟ 1, 12; V

Friendly staff serve great quality sashimi, *ponzu*-marinated *carpaccios* and a full range of rolls at this elegant Japanese restaurant. There's also a host of other standards from *gyoza* (dumplings) to soba and teppan-yaki and a decent vegetarian selection.

JUBIN *Chinese, Japanese, Southeast Asian*   €
☎ 02 349 0278; **Via Paolo Sarpi 11;** ✆ 6-11.30pm Mon-Sun; ⛟ 12, 14

Ultrapopular with groups of young Milanese, this reliable pan-Asian place serves generous pretty plates of fresh sashimi, interesting vegetable dishes such as stir-fried chilli broadbeans and a smattering of Thai and Vietnamese standards.

LA CANTINA DI MANUELA *Italian*   €€
☎ 02 345 2034; www.lacantinadi manuela.it; **Via Giulio Cesare Procaccini 41;** ✆ noon-3pm & 6pm-1am Mon-Sat; ⛟ 29, 30, 33

This Sempione branch of the well-known *enoteca* chain has a lovely light dining room and charming staff. (Also at Via Carlo Poerio 3, p119.)

CHINATOWN

Milan's Chinatown is centred on **Via Paolo Sarpi** and cross street, **Via Donato Bramante**. The Chinese community has deep roots in the city. More-recent arrivals mix with families that settled here in the 1920s and '30s, who have long since intermarried and consider themselves 'hyphenated'. While Milan likes to think of itself as Italy's most multicultural city, casual racism or the flip fetishism of fashion-land can be the most common response to questions of ethnic identity. Tensions exploded here in 2007, following police harassment of local textile workers, and a demonstration that turned into a riot was met with a disappointing flurry of anti-immigration sentiment from many Milanese. But hard work and harmony is the usual order of the day in Paolo Sarpi, as it's often referred to; the neighbourhood has a buzz that other areas of the city can only envy. It's a good shopping alternative for the glammed-out. Pick up bargain clothing, leatherwear and electrical goods, as well as Asian produce (there's even a fresh tofu shop). It's also known for its great value restaurants: Chinese, sushi and, increasingly, South-East Asian.

🍴 LA CANTINA DI VIA MUSSI
Enoteca €€
☎ 02 341459; Via Mussi 13;
🕑 closed Sun; 🚊 1, 29, 30
Eat *carpaccio* tuna or octopus and a well-priced bowl of pasta beneath shelf after shelf of wine at this sweet neighbourhood favourite.

🍴 L'ALTRA PHARMACIA
Italian, Enoteca €€
☎ 02 345 1300; www.laltrapharmacia.it; Via Antonio Rosmini 3; 🕑 noon-midnight Mon-Sun; Ⓜ Moscova
This rustic wine bar has extended kitchen hours and serves up hearty Milanese dishes to a happy band of locals and expats. Known for meat dishes, Friulian wines and, on a cold winter's night, its excellent range of grappa.

🍴 LYR *Lebanese* €€€
☎ 02 336 12 490; www.restaurant-lyr
.com; Corso Sempione 48; 🕑 noon-2.30pm & 7pm-midnight Tue-Fri & Sun, 7pm-midnight Sat; 🚊 1, 29, 30; Ⓥ
Like Milan, Beirut knows a thing or two about OTT style, and the chandeliers and Louis chairs make this a rather special place to feast on an authentic meze of *fattoush* (parsley and toasted bread salad), fish *kibbeh* (dumplings), *foul moudammes* (fava beans) and grilled beef skewers.

🍴 SERGIO & EFISIO
Cafe, Italian €
☎ 02 312319; Corso Sempione 32;
🕑 noon-2am Mon-Sat; 🚊 1, 19
Pull up a chair at this roadside tent for lunch with RAI worker bees or half of Milan after a night of

bar-hopping down the road. The *panini farciti* (stuffed roll), *spianata sarda* (round Sardegan bread) or olive oil–anointed slab of focaccia beats a burger hands down.

🍴 TRATTORIA DEGLI ORTI
Italian €€
☎ 02 331 01 800; Via Monviso 13; ☙ 7.30-10.30pm Mon-Sat; 🚋 12, 14
The menu is just a formality; dishes come along without prior consultation. Get ready for platters of gratined mussels, sardines *in saôr* (a sweet-and-sour onion jam), whitebait fritters, anchovy-stuffed zucchini flowers, homemade fish ravioli and crispy fried octopus. The lunchtime crowd of silver-haired, ties-off businessmen don't seem in the usual hurry to get back to work; the kitchen might have one more surprise in store.

🍴 TRIENNALE DESIGN CAFÉ
Cafe, Contemporary Italian €€
☎ 02 875441; www.triennale.it; Viale Alemanga 6; ☙ 10.30am-8.30pm Tue-Sun; Ⓜ Cadorna
Overlooking the Parco Sempione treetops, the Design Café is a large, white, light space with an open kitchen and fittings displaying suitable design cred. The food is fresh, modern Italian, though some dishes muddle north and south flavours (olives and walnut oil in a salad?) and staff can't seem to find the midpoint between chaos and inertia.

🍸 DRINK

🍸 BAR BIANCO *Bar*
☎ 02 869 92 026; www.bar-bianco.com; Parco Sempione; ☙ 7pm-1am Wed & Thu, 7pm-2am Fri & Sat; Ⓜ Lanza
Perennially popular, Bar Bianco is the most down-to-earth of the Parco bars. The patio seats are good for people-watching, but securing a seat on the upper terrace is the aim; it's like having a cocktail in a treehouse.

🍸 BHANGRA BAR
Bar, Live venue
☎ 02 349 34 469; www.bhangrabarmilano.com; Corso Sempione 1; ☙ 7pm-midnight Wed & Thu, 7pm-2am Fri, 10pm-2am Sat, 7-10pm Sun; 🚋 1, 29
Bhangra Bar is famous for its couscous-and-curry *aperitivo* buffet, served with a side of African percussion on Friday. Cushions, couches and earthy colours add to the chilled-out vibe.

🍸 CANTINE ISOLA *Bar, Enoteca*
☎ 02 331 5249; Via Paolo Sarpi 30; ☙ closed Mon; Ⓜ Garibaldi
Only octogenarians make use of the table in back – everyone else hovers near the beautiful old bar, balancing plates of *bruschetta* and

holding glasses at the ready for their selection of wines from 400 exceptional vintners.

☿ JUST CAVALLI CAFÉ *Bar*

☎ 02 311817; www.justcavallicafe.com; **Parco Sempione**; ⏱ 8pm-2am Mon-Sun; Ⓜ **Cadorna**

Tents, which are trussed up in Cavalli's key look for the season, create a camp carnival atmosphere under the Torre Branca. Yes, it's a circus and the strongmen at the door will decide whether you're allowed to join (tip: book for dinner).

☿ LIVING *Bar*

☎ 02 331 0084; www.livingmilano.com; **Piazza Sempione 2**; ⏱ 8-2am Mon-Fri, 9-2am Sat-Sun; Ⓜ **Moscova**

Living has one of the city's prettiest settings, with a corner position and floor-to-ceiling windows overlooking the Arco della Pace. You can grab a *dulce de leche*–smeared cornetto here for breakfast, but the action doesn't start till much later, when the bounteous *aperitivo* spread and expertly mixed cocktails draw crowds of smart-casual 20- and 30-somethings.

☿ MILANO *Bar*

☎ 02 365 36 060; **Via Procaccini 37**; ⏱ 6pm-2am Tue-Sat; 🚃 29, 30, 33

This popular bar shares owners with Roialto (opposite). It's smaller

VIA PARIGI

There's a certain Parisian air to Parco Sempione, which has more than a little to do with Napoleon. The beautiful **Arena**, on the park's northeastern boundary, was built in 1806 and opened by Napoleon with a chariot race. Luigi Cagnola's Paris-facing **Arco della Pace** (Arch of Peace), was also begun in 1807 in his honour, though was ironically only finished during the Austro-Hapsburg restoration in 1838.

and starker than Roialto (though still huge by any other standards), but bears many Roialto trademarks. There's vintage '60s and '70s furniture in black, white and orange, stacks – literally – of interiors magazines and the 'too much is never enough' *aperitivo*, with many items cooked to order.

☿ OLD FASHION CAFÉ *Bar, Club*

☎ 02 805 6231; www.oldfashion.it; **Parco Sempione**; ⏱ 9.30pm-4.30am; Ⓜ **Cadorna**

Wade through the furiously texting *figli di papa* (rich brats) and make it past the bouncers, and you'll be rewarded with an expansive outdoor bar that sits in the shadow of the Triennale and Parco Sempione trees. But with the *aperitivo* queues and an ultracommercial soundtrack, you'll need youth or supernatural stamina to make it to sunrise.

▼ ROIALTO *Bar*

☎ 02 349 36 616; Via Piero della Francesca 55; ⏱ closed Mon; 🚊 1,14,19, 33

This high-ceilinged former market is strewn with '70s sofas, interiors magazines and bright young things. The *aperitivo* here is famously unstinting, though the international hotel buffet breakfast vibe conjured by uniformed staff at twee stations (doling out oysters, artisan cheeses and whatever you damn well want) can hardly be cool, can it?

▼ SIDDHARTA BUDDHA CAFE *Bar*

☎ 02 336 19 183; www.siddhartacafe.com; Viale Elvezia 4; ⏱ 6.30-10pm Mon-Sun; Ⓜ Moscova

You can easily get lost under a pile of cushions in this big old hippy fantasy for those that were definitely not there first time round. Very chilled, except when the *aperitivo* platters appear.

▼ STALINGRADO *Pub*

☎ 02 331 9249; Via Ezio Biondi 4; ⏱ noon-3pm & 6.45pm-2am Mon-Sat; 🚊 1, 19, 33

The pub might be a popular notion in Milan but Stalingrado is one of the few that gets what a messy, beery proposition a pub

actually is. Scottish ale is on tap, football is on the big screen and a tented footpath area is erected for warmer nights. Milanese sports fans demand comfort as well as beer; you'll have to book for a set sit-down dinner to secure a viewing position for high-profile matches.

▼ WAGAMAGA *Bar*

☎ 02 341030; www.wagamaga.it; Via Saronno 1; ⏱ noon-midnight Tue-Sun; 🚊 1, 19, 33

Tucked away on a quiet street, Wagamaga can seem like an apparition with its New York diner facade. No homefries and brewed coffee on offer though. Just a nice local scene, simple snacks and well-priced drinks.

☆ PLAY

☆ GATTOPARDO *Club*

☎ 02 345 37 699; Via Piero della Francesca 47; ⏱ 6pm-4am Tue-Sun; 🚊 1,14,19, 33

Fashionable Milan worships commercial house music and BPM at this deconsecrated church with a bar where the altar once was. That mighty chandelier dangling from the cupola is mostly there for looks, but then the same can be said of the staff.

>CORSO COMO, PORTA GARIBALDI & ISOLA

Set on either side of the imposing Porta Garibaldi and the Piazzale XXV Aprile, Corso Garibaldi and Corso Como are synonymous with shopping and nightlife. During summer, the pedestrianised streets have a cruisey, southern-Californian feel. North of Garibaldi station is Isola, an island both by name and by nature; the walkway that straddles the seemingly endless train tracks may be far more desolate than Porta Genova's quaint graffiti bridge but affords spectacular urban views. Isola is not all post-industrial pregentrification warehouses; its squares and grand apartment buildings are home to a vibrant community of immigrants, artists, students and increasingly, young professionals. Come on a Saturday morning for the street market around Piazza Lagosta, it's colourful, cheap and a great way to experience Milan's much touted diversity. To the east is the city's main train station Stazione Centrale. This area has a large Middle Eastern, African and Indian population and many cheap eating options, budget hotels and a small, low-key gay nightclub strip. It *can* be seedy late at night, but gets a lot of undeserved hysterical press.

CORSO COMO, PORTA GARIBALDI & ISOLA

◎ SEE
Galleria Carla
  Sozzani.....................1 B3
Galleria Lia Rumma........2 B4
Monica de Cardenas
  Galleria.....................3 C3
Stazione Centrale...........4 E2
Torre Pirelli 5 E3

🏠 SHOP
10 Corso Como.............(see 1)
10 Corso Como
  Outlet 6 B2
Anthias 7 D3

ASAP......................8 B4
Boule de Neige...........9 B3
Showroom Isola 10 B2

🍽 EAT
10 Corso Como
  Café ....(see 1)
Antica Trattoria
  della Pesa 11 B3
Cantiere dei Sensi......12 B2
Ex Mauri 13 C2
Princi 14 B3
Teatro7 ....15 B1

🍸 DRINK
Chinese Box...............16 B4
Frida....................17 B2
Moscatelli...............18 B4
Nordest Caffé 19 B1
Radetzky Café 20 B4

★ PLAY
Anteospazio Cinema 21 B4
Blue Note...............22 B1
Gasoline Club 23 B3
Hollywood..............24 B3
Nuova Idea 25 C2
Shocking Club 26 B4

👁 SEE

◉ GALLERIA CARLA SOZZANI

☎ 02 653531; www.galleriacarlasozzani
.org; Corso Como 10; ⏱ 3.30-7.30pm
Mon, 10.30am-7.30pm Tue & Fri-Sun,
10.30am-9pm Wed & Thu; Ⓜ Garibaldi
This simple, light gallery space has
a good programme of high-
profile photographic shows that
fall all the way along the design-
art continuum.

◉ GALLERIA LIA RUMMA

☎ 02 290 00 101; www.gallerialiarumma
.it; Via Solferino 44; ⏱ 11am-1pm &
3-7pm Tue-Sat; Ⓜ Moscova
In an inversion of north–south
convention, this is the Milanese
outpost of Lia Rumma's Neapolitan gallery. An early collector of
Arte Povera, Rumma's curatorial
vision is legend and her international stable impressive: Marina
Abromovic, Anslem Kiefer, Andreas
Gursky and Peter Halley. She also
shows high-profile Italians – look
out for Ottonella Mocelli, Franco
Scognamiglio and increasingly
queasy-making Vanessa Beecroft.

◉ MONICA DE CARDENAS GALLERIA

☎ 02 290 10 068; www.artnet.com
/decardenas.html; Via Francesco Viganó
4; ⏱ 3-7pm Tue-Sat; Ⓜ Moscova
A contemporary gallery that shows
conceptual work, including some
interesting photographic artists.

◉ STAZIONE CENTRALE

Piazza Duca d'Aosta; Ⓜ Centrale FS
Annually, nearly 100 million
people pass through these hulking
portals onto train platforms beneath a cinematic cylindrical glass
roof. Begun in 1912 but finally realised between 1925 and 1931, the
extraordinary design is flush with
the nationalist fervour that marked
Mussolini's rule. Most of the overtly
Fascist symbolism was removed
or obscured but the Deco-tinged
neo-Babylonian architecture can
hardly hide its intent.

Stazione Centrale

WORTH THE TRIP: HANGAR BICOCCA

To the north-east of the city centre is this stunning, multipurpose exhibition space of **Hangar Bicocca** (☎ 02 8535 31764; www.hangarbicocca.it; Via Chiese 2; ⏱ 11am-7pm Tue, Wed & Fri-Sun, 2.30-10pm Thu; Ⓜ Sesto Marelli), in a vast industrial site that once was the heart of the Pirelli company's operations. Its smartly curated temporary shows are certainly worth a look, but the big, and we mean big, attraction is a permanent installation by German artist Anselm Kiefer. The seven concrete-and-lead towers of *The Seven Heavenly Palaces* are a teetering 15m tall, tucked under the dark blue canopy of the 7000-sq-metre space. The precarious, ruined shells invoke the mythical, mystical yearning of their title as well as the abject destruction of postwar Europe.

◉ TORRE PIRELLI
Pirellone; Piazza Duca d'Aosta 3;
Ⓜ **Centrale FS**
Construction began in 1956 on Milan's tallest *grattacielo* (skyscraper). The 32-storied Pirelli Tower sits on the site of the company's 19th-century factory, symbolically bookending Italy's industrial heyday. The smooth tapered sides of Gio Ponti's modernist icon form the shape of a diamond, his oft-used graphic trademark.

SHOP

⬛ 10 CORSO COMO *Fashion, Bookshop*
☎ 02 290 02 674; www.10corsocomo
.com; Corso Como 10; ⏱ 3.30-7.30pm Mon, 10.30am-7.30pm Tue & Fri-Sun, 10.30am-9pm Wed & Thu; Ⓜ **Garibaldi**
It might be the world's most hyped 'concept shop', but Carla Sozzani's consistently clever selection of highly desirable things (Lanvin ballet flats, Alexander Girard wooden dolls, a flask of the smoky, oud-laden house perfume, a Marc Newson for Myla 'object', a demi-couture frock by a designer you've not read about *yet*) really does make 10 Corso Como Milan's most thrilling shopping experience. Next to the gallery upstairs there is an equally browsable bookshop with art and design titles, Bruno Munari children's books, magazines and a large music department.

⬛ 10 CORSO COMO OUTLET
Fashion, Menswear, Outlet
☎ 02 290 02 674; www.10corsocomo
.com; Via Tazzoli 3; ⏱ 1-7pm Fri, 11am-7pm Sat & Sun; 🚋 3, 4 Ⓜ **Garibaldi**
At the back of a sunny courtyard, you'll find a surprisingly serene outlet store. There are genuine bargains on big names like Marni, Prada and Comme, and even better discounts on quirkier pieces like Stephen Jones hats. Menswear is particularly strong.

WORTH THE TRIP: LAMBRATE

Milan's contemporary art scene needed a neighbourhood where the square-footage rates were less stratospheric and the mood remained grungy: hello Lambrate. The art core 'Zonaventura' lies across railway tracks from Lambrate metro, four stops on the green line from Stazione Centrale.

First up is the **Prometeogallery** (☎ 02 269 24 450; www.prometeogallery.com; Via Ventura 3) specialising in screen-based art. Further on, the multilevel gallery **Massimo de Carlo** (☎ 02 700 03 987; www.massimodecarlo.it; Via Ventura 5, rear bldg) is entered via a bridge that gives a full view of the stockroom innards. This Via Ventura pioneer is a must-see, for the stellar line-up of artists – Diego Perrone, Simone Berti, Pei-Ming Yan – as well as the architecturally thoughtful space. In the same complex is the ever-challenging **Zero** (www.galleria zero.it; Via Ventura 5, front bldg, upper level) and **Art Book Milano** (☎ 02 215 97 624; www .artbookmilano.it; Via Ventura 5). Via Massimiano is home to **Francesca Minini** (☎ 02 269 24 671; www.francescaminini.it; Via Massimiano 25) and **Klerkx** (☎ 02 215 97 763; www .manuelaklerkx.com; Via Massimiano 25), both showing intriguing new-generation work.

The offices for design publishers Domus and Abitare took over old factories and were joined by architectural firms and design showrooms. Plan your trip for gallery opening times – noon to 7.30pm (closed Monday) as there's no real after-hours scene. For sustenance, **Gelateria Chocolate** (☎ 02 873 83 603; Viale delle di Rimembranze 9) does *gelati*-filled brioche or go to **Birrificio** (☎ 02 706 38 678; www.birrificiolambrate.com; Via Adelchi 5) microbrewery.

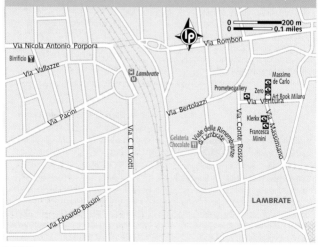

ANTHIAS *Jewellery*
☎ 02 670 0203; www.anthiasboom.com; Via Generale Gustavo Fara 33; ⏱ 10am-7pm Tue-Sat; Ⓜ Gioia

You know that wood and silver choker you loved at MoMA gift shop, and those bronze sea anemone earrings you adored in Shibuya, Tokyo? They're made right here in the Milan atelier of Monica Castiglioni (daughter of Achille Castiglioni) and Natsuko Toyofuku.

ASAP *Fashion*
☎ 02 659 8157; www.asaplab.it; Corso Garibaldi 104; ⏱ 3.30-7.30pm Mon, 10.30am-7.30pm Tue-Fri; Ⓜ Moscova

Locally sourced, recycled jersey, cashmere and leather are the base materials of asap (as sustainable as possible). The pieces are not just gorgeously detailed, cool and unique; they question fashion's endlessly recurring cycle of excitement and oblivion. What else would a smart girl wear?

BOULE DE NEIGE *Fashion*
☎ 02 629 10 777; Corso Como 3; ⏱ 10am-6pm Tue-Sat; Ⓜ Garibaldi

Such a small, wonderfully edited selection of shoes, accessories, separates and dresses makes pulling out the credit card too easy. Emma Hope's distressed metallic runners and/or Boule de Neige's own brand of cashmere cardies and patterned silk smocks? In

which colour? Staff are sweet and utterly unfazable.

SHOWROOM ISOLA
Fashion, Menswear
☎ 02 873 90 245; www.isoladellamoda.info; Via Carmagnola 7; ⏱ 11am-8pm Mon-Sat; Ⓜ Garibaldi

Functioning as a gallery, ideas laboratory *and* shop, this creative hotspot sells very limited editions handmade clothes and homewares. A rare Milanese champion of the iconoclastic DIY aesthetic, it also stocks what might be the city's most ironic souvenir T-shirts.

EAT

10 CORSO COMO CAFÉ
Café €€€
☎ 02 290 13 581; www.10corsocomo.com; Corso Como 10; ⏱ 12.30pm-midnight Mon-Fri, 11.30-1.30am Sat & Sun; Ⓜ Garibaldi

A picture-perfect courtyard space, world-class people-watching and thoughtful touches (a plate of crisp vegetable crudités and extra virgin comes with grissini before the meal) make up for the occasional lacklustre dish and service. Plus it offers the ultimate in afternoon tea: your choice of caviar and blinis (from €55) and a pot of Mariage Frères tea. The circular bar inside is a great place for a glass of wine.

🍴 ANTICA TRATTORIA DELLA PESA *Italian* €€€

☎ 02 655 5741; Viale Pasubio 10;
🕐 12.30-2.30pm & 7.30-11pm Mon-Sat;
🚋 3, 4

A recipe for instant nostalgia: take the landmark building where Ho Chi Minh stayed in the '30s, add literary types from nearby publishing houses, mix with comfort food – osso bucco on polenta topped with gremolata, *bollito misto* (boiled meat) and *cotoletta* (crumbed veal cutlets) – spice it up with some red, and finish with a sigh and smooth, boozy zabaglione.

🍴 CANTIERE DEI SENSI *Contemporary Italian* €€

☎ 02 668 03 446; www.cantieredei sensi.it; Via Carmagnola 5; 🕐 6.45pm-1am Tue-Fri, 7.30pm-2am Mon & Sat;
Ⓜ Garibaldi

Part bar, part restaurant, part showroom, this corner of Isola is symbolic of the winds of change but retains a neighbourhood feel. Food is fresh and simple with re-gional touches and a flexible menu that works well with wine; ignore the design posturing and relax.

🍴 EX MAURI *Italian, Venetian* €€

☎ 02 608 56 028; www.exmauri.com; Via Federico Confalonieri 5;
🕐 noon-3pm & 6-11pm Mon-Fri,
6-11pm Sat; Ⓜ Garibaldi

Go to this contemporary, stylish Venetian *bacaro* (bar) on Milan's urban island when you need a little Lombard-free time. Pull up a school chair at a lovingly scuffed table for imaginative seafood *cicheti* (Venetian-style tapas): *baccalà* fritters, sardines in *saôr* (sweet-and-sour onion jam) and braised baby octopus. Smart but hearty mains take their cues from both Venice and further afield, while the *gelati* and cakes are house-made.

🍴 PRINCI *Bakery* €

☎ 02 290 60 832; www.princi.it; Piazza XXV Aprile 5; 🕐 7-2am;
Ⓜ Moscova, Garibaldi

Not all Princi branches are created equal. This one is blessed with the same beautiful Claudio Silvestrin design as its Via Speronari sister (p54), and is open similarly long hours, giving you lots of opportuni-ties to sample their artisan range.

🍴 TEATRO 7 *Contemporary Italian, Cooking class* €€€

☎ 02 890 73 719; www.teatro7.com;
Via Thaon di Revel 7; 🕐 office 1-6.30pm Mon-Fri; Ⓜ Zara

Rock-star chef Rico Guarnieri is yours, as he blurs boundaries be-tween kitchen and table, cook and diner. Make a meal with the best local seasonal produce using tradi-tional techniques, set the table and eat. The space is a fabulous combi-nation of dream kitchen and slick

Rico Guarnieri
Teatro 7 & Giorgio Armani's private chef

Where did you learn to cook? I've been a set designer, I've written books and made TV shows... I learnt to cook watching my mother. **What does Milan taste like?** The yellow rice! Risotto with saffron, and *cotoletta* – I never eat them anywhere else; it's what I ate growing up. **Your culinary philosophy?** I want people to taste all the ingredients, every one. Use the best ingredients and keep it simple. When the good ingredients get together, there's an explosion. **What do you eat on your night off?** I work like 18 hours every day, so it's usually a late night panini from Sergio & Efisio (p96). **Favourite part of the city?** Isola – because it's a little city of its own, with flower sellers, bakers, people saying *ciao*; it's real. **Favourite drink?** My own mojito – I muddle Ligurian basil instead of mint.

shop-front dining room. There's a kids' afternoon on Saturday; call for details and bookings.

DRINK

CHINESE BOX *Bar*
☎ 02 655 4564; Corso Garibaldi 104; 🕒 8-2am Mon-Sun; Ⓜ Moscova
A small, friendly WYSIWYG bar that lets you face off with the Radesky crowd when you're not in the mood to dress up. Run by hip Chinese-Italian twins who know that sometimes a cold beer, a bowl of *patatine fritte* (crisps) and a smile is all you really need.

FRIDA *Bar*
☎ 02 680260; www.fridaisola.it; Via Pollaiuolo 3; 🕒 6pm-2am Mon-Sun; Ⓜ Zara, Garibaldi
The jumble of tables in the heated courtyard and comfy couches inside make it easy to bond over beer or regional wine with an arty crowd. The *aperitivo* spread is continuously replenished and sports plenty of veg dishes. No pretensions, no entourages, just good music, good value and good times.

MOSCATELLI *Enoteca*
☎ 02 655 4602; Corso Garibaldi 93; 🕒 8-1am Mon-Sat; Ⓜ Moscova
It may have been open since the Franco-Austrian war, but the decor at this popular bar belongs firmly in the 1950s. It's all about the wine,

and maybe a plate of *coppa* (cured pork neck) and some bread.

NORDEST CAFFÉ *Bar*
☎ 02 690 01 910; www.nordestcaffe.it; Via Borsieri 35; 🕒 8am-1.30pm Mon, 8am-midnight Tue-Sat, 8.30am-10pm Sun; Ⓜ Garibaldi, Zara
So laid-back you might have trouble getting served, this sunny cafe-bar invites long, lazy afternoons. The young, local crowd have that down to an art, especially for Sunday brunch from midday, when the live jazz begins.

RADETZKY CAFÈ *Bar*
☎ 02 657 2645; Corso Garibaldi 105; 🕒 8am-1am; Ⓜ Moscova
Fabulous banquette and window seating make it one of the most popular places in this strip for *aperitivo* or long Sunday sessions (well, it started with brunch…). The tanned, tarted-up crowd spills onto the street. The cakes and *cotoletta* are justifiably famous.

PLAY

ANTEOSPAZIO CINEMA *Cinema*
☎ 02 659 7732; www.spaziocinema.info; Via Milazzo 9; Ⓜ Moscova
On rainy Mondays, take your pick of three screens showing original-language films, from classics to indies, then loiter in the bookshop, restaurant and exhibition space.

⊞ BLUE NOTE *Jazz*
☎ 899 700 022; www.bluenotemilano
.com; Via P Borsieri 37; ⏱ 7.30pm-2am
Tue-Sat (2 shows nightly; prices vary),
7.30-11pm Sun; Ⓜ Zara, Garibaldi
It's jazz at the Blue Note alright, and
this branch of the New York venue
has the acoustics and two-shows-
a-night tradition to prove it. The
programme is broad; the crème
of European players, US legends,
and soul and R&B artists from Terry
Callier to Robin Thicke.

⊞ GASOLINE CLUB *Club*
☎ 334 757 7441; www.discogasoline.it;
Via Bonnet 11a; ⏱ 11pm-4am Thu & Sat,
midnight-4am Fri, 6-11pm Sun;
Ⓜ Garibaldi
Everything seems larger than life
in this diminutive disco, which
is marginally more democratic
than many of the other Garibaldi
venues. Nights include Thursday's
electro grunge Popstartz, Friday's
techno/house Queen and Saturday's disorderly Disorder.

⊞ HOLLYWOOD *Club*
☎ 02 659 8996; www.discotecaholly
wood.it; Corso Como 15; ⏱ 10.30pm-
2am Tue-Sun; Ⓜ Garibaldi
This is the club frequented by footballers and supermodels, and those
that come to gawk at them. If you
make it in, you might see the next
scandal in the making, or you might
wonder what the fuss is about.

⊞ LEONCAVALLO
Live music venue
☎ 02 670 5621; www.leoncavallo.org;
Via Watteau 7; Ⓜ 5, 7
Begun in the red-or-dead '70s,
and proving to be one of the
most resilient of the *centri sociali*
(anarcho-socialist cultural organisations), Leoncavallo hosts electronic
evenings and live gigs that attract
large, alternative crowds. Check the
website for details (just in case the
bulldozers got there first).

⊞ NUOVA IDEA *Club*
☎ 02 690 07 859; www.lanuovaidea.com;
Via Gaetano de Castilla 30; ⏱ 10.30pm-
3am Thu-Sun; Ⓜ Gioia
Go club-hopping without leaving
this many-splendoured nightlife
theme park, one of Milan's premier
gay clubs since 1975. One room
features ballroom dancing, the
next cages with greased-up gogo
dancers. At the centre of it all, celebrated transvestites put Fashion
Week runway shows to shame.

⊞ SHOCKING CLUB *Club*
☎ 02 626 90 045; www.shockingclub.net;
Bastioni di Porta Nuova 12; ⏱ 11.30pm-
4am Tue-Sat; Ⓜ Moscova
A huge and hugely popular club
that hosts various nights; DJs spin
everything from '80s schlock to
commercial house to hip-hop. And
remember, the spots were there
before you started in on the Stoli.

>SAN BABILA

Beyond the shops, towering Fascist architecture and frenetic traffic of Piazza San Babila, most of the city's famed interior design showrooms cluster along Via San Damiano, Via Durini, Corso Monforte and Porta Vittoria. There's quite a few civic buildings here too, many with Fascist architectural heritage, including Milan's law courts, the Palazzo di Giustizia. Bustling during the day, they come over all Di Chirico in the evening and on weekends. The intensely dramatic monument in Piazza Cinque Giornate celebrates Milan's five days in the revolutionary sun in 1848 (see p175). Further east, around the Piazza Tricolore and Piazza Risorgimento, understated, upmarket residential streets are dotted with interesting small shops, bars and restaurants. Towards the Giardini Pubblici, you can see some of Milan's most extraordinarily grand Novecento and Liberty apartment buildings. Look up for a glimpse of spectacular roof gardens. Pier Portaluppi's Villa Nechi-Campiglio nestles among them in Via Mozart, while just around the corner on Via Serbelloni you'll find an enormous grey marble ear jutting from the Casa Sola-Busca. Designed by Adolfo Wildt, it was once the resident's entry phone. Surreal, but so Milan.

SAN BABILA

⊙ SEE

Galleria Christian Stein ..1 B2
San Babila 2 A2
Studio Giangaleazzo
    Visconti ....(see 1)
Villa Necchi Campiglio ...3 B1

🛍 SHOP

B&B Italia 4 A3
Cappellini 5 A2
Cassina 6 A3
ė De Padova.....................7 A1

Flos 8 A2
Guzzini 9 A1
Il Salvagente 10 E2
L'Altro Vino 11 C1
L'Arte di Offrire il Thé ...12 E2
Lula Cioccolato 13 D3
MH Way 14 A2
Mihai 15 E2
Nava 16 A3
Olivo 17 D1
Teo 18 D2
W Fiori 19 D2
Zanotta..........................20 C2

🍴 EAT

California Bakery...........21 C2
Da Giacomo 22 D2
Eataly 23 C4
Gold 24 D1
Sissi...............................25 D2

🍸 DRINK

Cantina de Manuela 26 D1
La Belle Aurore.............27 E1

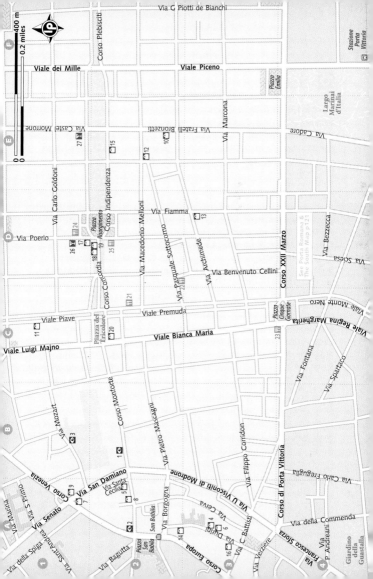

⦿ SEE

⦿ GALLERIA CHRISTIAN STEIN

☎ 02 763 93 301, 02 795251; **Corso Monforte 23;** ⌚ **10am-7pm Tue-Fri; 10am-1pm & 3-7pm Sat;** Ⓜ San Babila
Artists shown here include Arte Povera proponents such as Mario Merz and Alighiero Boetti and Transavantgardist Mimmo Paladino.

⦿ SAN BABILA

☎ 02 760 02 877; www.sanbabila.org; **Piazza San Babila;** ⌚ **8am-noon & 3.30-7pm;** Ⓜ San Babila
Built on the site of a 2nd-century pagan temple, this squat church has suffered at the hands of over-zealous renovators (the last add-on being the Neo-Romanesque facade and bell tower early last century). Still, it exerts a calm force amid the swirling visual din of supersized billboards, office blocks and ever-flowing traffic of the piazza, and its lily-scented interior is a serene respite. The Venetian lion-topped column at the entrance dates back to 1656.

⦿ STUDIO GIANGALEAZZO VISCONTI

☎ 02 795251; www.studiovisconti.net; **Corso Monforte 23; 11.30am-7.30pm Tue-Sat;** Ⓜ San Babila
This gallery is in the former studio of Lucio Fontana and has a similar stable of conceptual and Arte Povera artists as Christian Stein (left), who shares the building.

⦿ VILLA NECCHI CAMPIGLIO

☎ 02 763 40 121; **Via Mozart 12; admission €6 (by guided tour only);** ⌚ **10am-6pm Wed-Sun (last entry 5.30pm);** Ⓜ San Babila
Set in a huge garden with a swimming pool, tennis court and tall magnolia trees, this 1932 Piero Portaluppi–designed house is a symbol of the city's industrial wealth and modernist imaginings. The superbly refurbished interiors are redolent of the Necchi sisters' privileged lifestyle, with a profu-

IDROSCALO IDYLL

Once the liquid landing strip for seaplanes, this **artificial lake** (☎ 02 702 00 902; www .provincia.milano.it/idroscalo; Via Circonvallazione Idroscalonear, Linate Airport) is now a summer playground. Concerts regularly take place here, including indie-leaning festivals, and there's swimming and water sports including wakeboarding and kite surfing. Check the website for details and a weekly calendar of events. Like its fellow little 'waterfront', Navigli, mosquitoes come to play, too – make sure you have good insect repellent. To get to Idroscalo, take bus 73 from San Babila to Linate Airport, then take the free shuttle.

Stare, with just a hint of jealousy, at the wealth of Villa Necchi Campiglio

sion of intriguing domestic detail, while the walls are hung with a collection of 20th-century Italian paintings. The garden restaurant opens until 9pm most evenings.

SHOP

B&B ITALIA *Furniture, Design*
☎ 02 764441; www.milano.bebitalia.com; Via Durini 14; ⏱ 10am-7pm Tue-Sat, 3-7pm Mon; Ⓜ San Babila
Antonio Citterio designed this new space for B&B and it makes a slick, simple backdrop for the company's ever-changing tableau of furniture and objects. Moooi's lifesize barnyard-animal tables get acquainted with Mario Bellini's reissued classic Bambole sofa.

CAPPELLINI *Furniture, Design*
☎ 02 778 07 701; www.cappellini.it; Via Santa Cecilia 4; ⏱ 2.30-7pm Mon, 10am-1.30pm & 2.30-7pm Tue-Sat; Ⓜ San Babila
Cappellini's drama-filled main showroom is nestled away on the road to Como, but its Milan shop is no less an assault of what Italian design is all about: colour, expressive forms and luxury materials.

CASSINA *Furniture, Design*
☎ 02 760 20 745; www.cassina.com; Via Durini 18; ⏱ 10am-7pm Tue-Sat; Ⓜ San Babila
In an excitable moment you could say *sì* and ship home Gió Ponti's 1955 classic *superleggera*

(superlight) chair. But even without booking container space, this showroom is a head rush for the design-conscious traveller. What a thrill to see, touch and plonk your bum on a Charles Rennie MacIntosh, Charlotte Perriand and Mario Bellini.

È DE PADOVA
Homewares, Design

☎ 02 777201; www.depadova.it; **Corso Venezia 14;** Ⓜ **Montenapoleone**
America's great modernist designer George Nelson called this shop 'one of the most beautiful in the world' and who are we to disagree? Maddalena De Padova's excellent eye has held sway here since 1965, and with six floors of great design to behold, it's a grand alternative to taking in all the showrooms if you're short of time or patience.

EATALY *Food, Wine*
02 928 70 066; www.eataly.it; **1st fl, Coin Bldg, Piazza Cinque Giornate;** Ⓣ **10am-8pm;** Ⓡ **12, 23, 27**
With a noble declaration of 'we understand that the conviviality around a laid table helps generate moments of true happiness', Turin's Slow Food supermarket has opened an outlet in Milan. Eataly aims to keep the supply chain simple, ensuring reasonable prices on artisan and small producer lines of wine, cheese, pasta, oils and even tuna. True happiness indeed.

SAY CHEESE
Milan may have gone mozzarella-mad, with the milky buffalo balls on their way from Campania every morning, but Lombardy's lush green pastures and alpine meadows have long produced magnificent cheeses of their own. Here's a sample of the region's famous softies:
Gorgonzola blue, intense, complicated, piquant
Taleggio runny, stinky, deceptively mild
Stracchino milk-sweet, rich, marvellous when melted
Mascarpone creamy, subtly tangy, sublime super fresh

FLOS *Homewares, Design*
☎ 02 760 01 641; www.flos.com; **Corso Monforte 9;** Ⓣ **3-7pm Mon, 10am-7pm Tue-Fri;** Ⓜ **San Babila**
From the playful modernism of Castiglioni's Taraxacum (dandelion) to the postmodern play in Marcel Wanders' Skygarden, Flos' innovative offerings are always the high point of Milan's lighting design fair, Euroluce. See for yourself at their Monforte showroom.

GUZZINI *Homewares*
☎ 02 762 1161; www.fratelliguzzini .com; **Via San Damiano 3;** Ⓣ **9am-1pm & 2-6pm Mon-Fri;** Ⓜ **San Babila**
Every Italian home has at least one piece of this ultrapractical homewares brand, be it napkin holders, canisters or a breadbin.

IL SALVAGENTE
Fashion outlet
☎ 02 761 10 328; www.salvagente
milano.it; Via Fratelli Bronzetti 16;
⏱ 3-7pm Mon, 10am-12.40pm & 3-7pm
Tue, Thu & Fri, 10am-7pm Wed & Sat;
Ⓜ San Babila

As you scurry down through the grim courtyard to this basement shop, it can all feel a bit below board. Don't worry, it may be cash only but the stock is legit, if so tightly jammed together on rails that you'll wish you'd done a few upper-body workouts in preparation. Brands include giants Prada, D&G, Versace, Ferretti and Armani, and more unusual labels such as Teo Erre.

L'ALTRO VINO *Wine*
☎ 02 780147; Viale Piave 9;
⏱ 11.30am-7.30pm Tue-Sat;
Ⓜ Palestro

Courteous and knowledgeable staff will help you choose a bottle of wine from the special selection of small vineyard producers from all regions of Italy.

L'ARTE DI OFFRIRE IL THÉ
Tea
☎ 02 715442; www.artedelricevere.com;
Via Macedonio Melloni 35; ⏱ 3.30-
7.30pm Mon, 10am-1pm & 3.30-7.30pm
Tue-Sat; 🚊 9

Tea has a pretty difficult time in a coffee-obsessed town, but this

Check out why ē De Padova is known as one of the most beautiful shops in the world

feminine, celadon-walled boutique offers not just a wide range of fine leaf, but also teapots, caddies and cups, as well as guided tastings and cooking (with tea) classes.

LULA CIOCCOLATO
Chocolate

☎ 02 700 06 915; www.lulamilano.com; Via Fiamma 17; ⏱ 4-8.30pm Mon, 10.30am-2pm & 4-8.30pm Tue-Sat; 🚋 12, 27

In a city full of exquisite sweet things, hip and oh-so-pretty Lula is a standout. Purists prefer the simple slabs scattered with nuts or the jewel-coloured French jellies, while those of a more decorative bent snap up votive- and cornucopia-shaped chocolates. Flavours run from traditional to highly experimental. Seasonal creations include baroque Easter eggs and crystallised flowers for Christmas or St Valentines Day cakes, which really do make the heart beat faster. For extra gift oomph, there's vintage cotton pouches or gold-centred bowls to fill.

MARKET FORECAST

Food markets spring up twice weekly in most neighbourhoods and are a great place to put together meals with the freshest fruit, cheese and cured meats, as well as grabbing a shopper's snack from the *rosticce'ria* van. Most markets also sell a combination of kitchenwear, cheap clothing, and designer seconds. Milan also has some great vintage and collectibles markets, including the *nonno* of them all, the Mercatone del Naviglio Grande.

Mercatone del Naviglio Grande (⏱ last Sun of the month; Ⓜ Porta Genova) Antiques, collectibles, second-hand clothing
Piazza Gramsci (⏱ 1st Sun of the month; 🚋 1, 12, 14, 19, 33) Crafts, organic food market
Piazzale Lagosta (⏱ Sat; Ⓜ Zara) Clothing, food
Piazza Wagner (⏱ Mon-Sat; Ⓜ Wagner) Food
Via Armorari (Piazza Cordusio; ⏱ Sun; Ⓜ Cordusio) Collectibles, postcards

Via Corsico, Naviglio Grande (⏱ last Sun of the month; Ⓜ Porta Genova) Twentieth-century vintage clothing
Via Fauche (⏱ Tue & Sat; 🚋 1, 12, 14, 19, 33) Clothing, designer seconds, food
Via Fiori Chiari (⏱ 3rd Sat & Sun of the month; Ⓜ Lanza) Antiques, collectibles
Via Lorenzini (⏱ Sun am; Ⓜ Lodi) Collectibles, secondhand clothing
Viale Papiniano (⏱ Tue am & Sat; Ⓜ Sant'Agostino) Designer seconds, food, secondhand clothing
Via San Marco (⏱ Mon am & Thu; Ⓜ Moscova) Clothing, designer seconds, food

▢ MH WAY *Accessories, Design*
☎ 02 760 21 727; www.mhway.it;
Via Durini 5; ⏰ 3-7pm Mon, 10am-7pm
Tue-Fri, 10am-2pm & 3-7pm Sat;
Ⓜ San Babila

Japanese designed, made-in-Milan bags known for their ingeniously compact shapes, sensational colours, technology-enhanced durability and prices.

▢ MIHAI *Toy shop*
☎ 02 710 40 531; www.mihai.it;
Corso Indipendenza 14; ⏰ 10am-7pm
Tue, Thu-Sun; 🚃 9, 23

Wooden toys, puzzles, German crayons and Birkenstocks crowd the window of this tiny store. It's a plastic-tat free zone that knows kids have good taste, too.

▢ NAVA *Accessories, Design*
☎ 02 794599; www.navadesign.com;
Via Durini 23; Ⓜ San Babila

The Milan-based designer's showroom displays well-priced office supplies and leather goods as well as occasional shows of painting and design. Products include great pocket notebooks and satchels that are good to go from office to gallery opening.

▢ OLIVO *Food*
☎ 02 365 66 091; www.olivoweb.com;
Piazza Risorgimento 3; ⏰ 9.30am-1pm
& 3-8pm Mon-Fri, 10.30am-2.30pm &
3.30-8pm Sat; 🚃 9

Extra virgin olive oil is sourced from small regional producers around the country and beautifully packaged in containers big and small. It also finds its way into aromatic oils and luscious cosmetics.

▢ TEO *Children's wear*
☎ 02 760 03 418; Corso Concordia 9;
⏰ 10am-1pm & 3.30-7.30pm Tue-Sat;
🚃 9, 23

A refreshingly unfussy and individual children's and babywear shop with a lovely range of bright and earth toned smocks, handmade toys and the sweetest Mary Jane shoes.

▢ W FIORI *Flowers*
☎ 02 365 30 346; Corso Concordia 11;
3.30-7.30pm Mon, 10am-1pm &
3.30-7.30pm Tue-Sat; Ⓜ San Babila

A bunch of shocking pink peonies from this colourful, stylish florist will brighten a drab hotel room or delight a Milanese host.

▢ ZANOTTA *Furniture, Design*
☎ 02 760 16 445; www.zanotta.it;
Piazza del Tricolore 2; ⏰ 10am-7pm;
Ⓜ San Babila

Zanotta has worked with the best (Enzo Mari, Bruno Munari and Ettore Sottsass to name a few) but is most famous for bringing the body-hugging, structure-free *sacco*, or beanbag, to the world,

NEIGHBOURHOODS

SAN BABILA

bang on time for postbarricade debriefs. Also of the same vintage and still in production is the Quaderna table, launched by antidesign outfit Superstudio in 1970, and pointedly made in cheap, gridded laminate to express, ah, 'political disillusionment'. In comparison, current-day experimentation can come across as a little try-hard.

🍴 EAT

🍴 CALIFORNIA BAKERY
Bakery, Burgers €

☎ 02 760 11 492; www.californiabakery .it; Viale Premuda 44; ⏱ 7.30am-7.30pm Mon-Fri, 9am-7.30pm Sat & Sun, burger time 7.30pm-midnight Thu-Sun; 🚇 9, 23

It's not just expats that flock to this small cafe for brownies, bagels, cheesecake or late-night burgers. Even when you have the world's most envied food culture, every now and again *tu vuoi fare l'Americana.*

🍴 DA GIACOMO *Italian* €€€
☎ 02 760 23 313; www.dagiacomo ristorante.it; cnr Via Benvenuto Cellini & Pasquale Sottocorno; ⏱ 12.30-3pm & 7.30pm-midnight; 🚇 9, 23

This place may look like a ye-olde-worlde tourist trap but is perennially popular with Milanese movers and shakers. They come for the

sunny Tuscan vibe and fresh, simple pastas such as spaghetti with sea urchin or linguine with scampi and zucchini flowers, and the wonderful seasonal truffle dishes. Seafood is a feature, along with a killer Fiorentina steak.

🍴 GOLD
Contemporary Italian €€€

☎ 02 757 7771; www.dolcegabbanagold .it; Via Carlo Poerio 2a; ⏱ cafe 8am-6.30pm, lounge bar 7pm-2am, bistro 8am-2am (kitchen noon-midnight), restaurant 7.30-11pm; 🚇 9, 23

Dolce & Gabbana's shiny paean to excess will either enthral or appal depending on your mood (and perhaps who's paying). Mirror-topped tables mean you can, as the (British) Beat once bitterly suggested, watch yourself while you are eating. There's a 'healthy' menu for those that find the eating part of the above equation tricky, though it reads like an import from an old fashioned fat farm, all wholegrain spaghetti and steaming. Pastas in the bistro, on the other hand, are both interesting and reasonably priced – gold!

🍴 SISSI *Pasticceria* €

☎ 02 760 14 664; Piazza Risorgimento 6; ⏱ closed Mon afternoon & Tue; 🚇 9, 23

You'll be on first name terms with the staff before you know it at this friendly French-speaking neighbourhood *pasticceria* that has some of the best and most varied breakfast brioche in town. There's a tiny garden at the back for Sunday brunches. Tarts, both sweet and savoury, are made with love and will be carefully wrapped to make a picnic lunch or hotel supper.

DRINK

CANTINA DI MANUELA
Enoteca
☎ 02 763 18 892; www.lacantinadi manuela.it; Via Poerio 3; ⏰ 11-1.30am Mon-Sat; 🚋 9, 23
Locals come after work to pick up a bottle of regional wine or share a generous platter of goat's cheese,

honey and *mostarda* over a glass while their kids munch on bread and draw. The kitchen kicks in around 7pm – what better excuse to try another varietal? Staff aren't as welcoming as the decor is inviting, but once you hear that bottle of Gavi di Gavi go glug-glug-glug, you'll feel right at home regardless.

LA BELLE AURORE *Bar*
☎ 02 294 06 212; Via Castel Morrone 1; ⏰ 8.30-2am Mon-Sat; Ⓜ San Babila; 🚋 9, 23
A local favourite, this old-style bar recalls the city of Buenos Aires. It attracts a laid-back, diverse crowd from breakfast through to *aperitivo* to late-night wine-soaked chats.

>PORTA ROMANA & THE SOUTH

Corso di Porta Romana runs southeast from Piazza Missori, past the Universitá Statale and on to Porta Romana, one of the city gates originally built by Barbarossa in the 12th century, on the ancient road to Rome. The tree-lined residential streets are filled with a number of grand *palazzi*, and also with good-value dining options catering to the students from neighbouring Bocconi, Milan's main business and economics university. Beyond the English-style Parco Ravizza, large swaths of old warehouses are being converted into office parks and new apartment complexes, some with more architectural merit than others. This neighbourhood is set for further redevelopment when the Prada Foundation opens its ambitious multipurpose space in 2011. The area's already one of Milan's late-night hot spots, home to some of its best bars, clubs and live venues but, despite the large number of places to go out (and they continue to pop up along Via Ripamonti and beyond) there's no real centre or scene.

PORTA ROMANA & THE SOUTH

◉ SEE
Fondazione Prada **1** D2
Fondazione Prada
   (future site) **2** D4
Galleria Emi Fontana **3** B3

🛍 SHOP
Danese **4** B1
Etro Outlet **5** D1

Puma Outlet **6** C2

🍴 EAT
Dar El Yacout **7** E1
Fingers **8** D3
Giulio Pane e Ojo **9** C3
Lacerba **10** C2
Maru **11** C3
Piccole Ischia **12** E2

🍸 DRINK
Volo **13** B3

⭐ PLAY
Magazzini Generali **14** B4
Plastic **15** E1
Rolling Stone **16** E1
Surfer's Den **17** D3
Teatro Carcano **18** B2

NEIGHBOURHOODS

PORTA ROMA & THE SOUTH

SEE
FONDAZIONE PRADA
☎ 02 541 92 230; www.fondazioneprada.org; Via Fogazzaro 36; ☾ 11am-8pm Tue-Sun during exhibition periods (check website for specific dates); Ⓜ Porta Romana

The Fondazione Prada produces two grand-scale, solo shows each year in an old warehouse that's impressive enough to give you 'art butterflies' on its own. The likes of Anish Kapoor and Louise Bourgeois, or mid-career mavericks such as Francesco Vezzoli and Nathalie Djurberg, do the space justice. Tours of the foundation's **new space** (☎ 02 535 70 9201; Largo Isarco 2; ☾ by appointment; Ⓜ Lodi), due to open in 2011, are held periodically. A wander in the world's most impressive stock room is worth the trip alone, but the official attraction is Rem Koolhaas' obsessively detailed maquettes and 2D renderings of the former brandy factory's brave new future.

GALLERIA EMI FONTANA
☎ 02 583 22 237; www.galleriaemifontana.com; Viale Bligny 42; ☾ 11am-7.30pm Tue-Sat; Ⓜ Porta Romana; 🚊 9, 29

This gallery shows challenging conceptual work by Italian artists Monica Bonvicini, Liliana Moro and Luca Vitone as well as Icelandic superstar Olafur Eliasson. A second gallery in LA makes for some interesting international collaborations.

SHOP
DANESE Design, Homewares
☎ 02 583 04 150; www.danesemilano.com; Piazza San Nazaro in Brolo 15; ☾ 2.30-7pm Mon, 10am-1.30pm & 2.30-7pm Tue-Sat; Ⓜ Crochetta

Milan's Danese may not be as well known as Piedmont's Alessi, but its products possess the same sense of wit and attention to everyday detail. If Enzo Mari's delightful Sea in a Box puzzle caught your eye at the Triennale Design Museum

LIGHT FANTASTIC
If you've ever contemplated the long desert drive to Marfa, Texas to see the work of American sculptor Dan Flavin, a metro trip to the end of the green line won't seem like too much of an effort. The suburban **Santa Maria Annunciata in Chiesa Rossa** (☎ 02 895 00 817; www.smacr.com; Via Neera 24; ☾ 9am-noon & 4-7pm; Ⓜ Abbiategrasso), an airy 1930s church, contains his last work, designed shortly before his death in 1996. The arrangement of red, yellow and blue fluorescent lights across the altar, apse and transept is a subtle work – the life and clutter of an everyday church goes on beneath it – but its mix of the formal and the emotional is all the more powerful for its setting.

(p94), then this is the place to make one your own.

🏬 ETRO OUTLET *Outlet*

☎ 02 550 20 218; Via Spartaco 3; ⏰ 3-7pm Mon, 10am-2pm & 3-7pm Tue-Sun; Ⓜ Porta Romana

The ultimate money look – silk ties, cashmere T-shirts, embellished purses and bolts of lavishly patterned fabric – at plebeian prices.

🏬 PUMA OUTLET *Outlet*

☎ 02 599 02 227; Viale Monte Nero 22; ⏰ 10am-8pm; Ⓜ Porta Romana

Sporty style for 40% less, including yoga wear, limited-edition pieces and Ferrari bags.

🍴 EAT

🍴 DAR EL YACOUT
Moroccan €€

☎ 02 546 2230; www.yacout.it; Via Cadore 23; ⏰ 5pm-2.30am; 🚋 9, 16

Take a North African style *aperitivo* at Yacout and you're on the slippery slope to a banquet dinner and a 1am spot of belly-dancing. This large space is lavishly decorated, mosaic-ed to the max and guarantees a good time.

🍴 FINGERS *Crudo, Italian* €€

☎ 02 541 22 675; Via San Gerolamo Emiliani 2; ⏰ 7-11pm Tue-Sun; Ⓜ Lodi

It's a very Milanese equation: 1 Brazilian chef + 1 Italian restaurateur = sushi. This moody, tatami-matted *ristorante* does a brisk trade in Italian-style *carpaccio*, sushi and squid-ink risotto to Nobu defectors wanting less attitude.

🍴 GIULIO PANE E OJO
Italian, Roman €€

☎ 02 545 6189; www.giuliopaneojo.com; Via Ludovico Muratori 10; ⏰ noon-2pm & 7-10.30pm Mon-Sat; Ⓜ Porta Romana

If all the Roman restaurants in town were this appealing, Milan would probably start calling itself Mediolanum (see p174) again. Waiters dish up Roman sass le at

Go North African style at Dar el Yacout

when asked to help you choose between the *bucatini amatriciana* (tube pasta with tomato, pecorino cheese and pig's cheek) and *salt-imbocca* (veal with sage). At these prices, why not try both?

🍴 LACERBA *Contemporary Italian* €€
☎ 02 545 5475; www.lacerba.it; Via Orti 4; ⏰ noon-3pm & 6.30pm-midnight Mon-Fri, 6.30pm-midnight Sat; Ⓜ Lamarmora Romana, Porta Romana

A homage to futurism, Milan's most infamous art movement, Lacerba has dishes from futurist Marinetti's kooky culinary manifesto (death to pasta!), as well as a less artistically strident repertoire of Mediterranean seafood. To counter all the violence, speed and surging machinery on the walls, there's also an excellent wine selection.

🍴 MARU *Japanese* €€€
☎ 02 583 28 501; www.maru.co.it; Viale Sabotino 19; ⏰ 7pm-midnight; Ⓜ Porta Romana

Roppongi alt-chic abounds in architect Anna Giorgi's design, and the aesthetic is reflected in the food and the diners. The extensive menu of soba, ramen, tempura and raw sets is joined by creative takes on the roll – Red Dragon combines spicy raw prawns and salmon eggs, while Green Eel adds

rocket and avocado to crisp grilled eel. Saketini, anyone?

🍴 PICCOLA ISCHIA *Pizzeria* €
☎ 02 541 07 410; www.piccolaischia.it; Viale Umbria 60; ⏰ noon-2.30pm & 7-11.30pm; Ⓜ Lodi, 🚋 16

Just like the Porta Venezia branch (p72), Neapolitan pizza served without fuss.

🍸 DRINK

🍸 VOLO *Bar*
☎ 02 583 25 543; Viale Beatrice d'Este 40; ⏰ noon-2.30pm, 6pm-2am Mon-Fri, 6pm-2am Sat-Sun; Ⓜ Porta Romana

Set behind a large iron gate in a typical Milanese house, Volo's courtyard is a pleasant place for a summer lunch (a €10 buffet makes it even more attractive) or *aperitivo* and excellent cocktails with a suited after-work crowd.

⭐ PLAY

⭐ CASA 139′ *Club, Live venue*
www.lacasa139.com; Via Ripamonti 139; Ⓜ Lodi

A small intimate space that features contemporary Italian songwriters as well as international acts. This is an ARCI club (Italian Recreative and Cultural Association) that requires a €13 membership, but non-Italians might be able to wangle their way in without one.

Gaia Polloni
DJ/Music Promoter

Where do you work? Mainly at Plastic; we host a different band from abroad every week. **Best place to see local bands?** If you wanna find good local bands, you better forget Milan! Italian bands do play Casa 139' (opposite) but it's a pretty rare event. Surfer's Den (p126) often have locals too and VERY good DJs but they have to keep their volume low as otherwise the police are called. **What song always reminds you of the city?** 'Asphalt World' by Suede. **What neighbourhood do you live in and what's the best thing about it?** I live close to Navigli. You can walk along the canals and jump from pub to pub for a beer, then to a music shop, a vintage shop, and a comics shop, too. It's young and alternative. **Describe Milan's nightlife:** Sleepless!

⭐ MAGAZZINI GENERALI
Club, Live venue

☎ 02 552 11 313; Via Pietrasanta 14; ⏰ 10pm-4am Wed-Sun; Ⓜ Lodi

When this former warehouse is full of people working up a sweat to an international indie act, there's no better place to be in Milan. Can't argue with the price: most gigs are under €20, and there's free entry on other nights when DJs get the party started.

⭐ PLASTIC *Club*

☎ 02 733996; www.thisisplastic.com; Viale Umbria 120; ⏰ 10pm-4am Tue-Sun; Ⓜ Lodi

In a fickle, unforgiving town, Plastic is still the club on everyone's lips after 25 decadent years. Friday's London Loves takes no prisoners with an edgy, transgressive indie mix and Milan's coolest kids. If you're looking fab, club art director Nicola Guiducci's private Match á Paris on a Saturday night mashes French pop, indie and avant-garde sounds or get down to hilarious '80s Italo disco and electro in the main room's Bordello.

⭐ ROLLING STONE
Bar, Live venue

☎ 02 733172; www.rollingstone.it; Corso XXII Marzo 32; ⏰ 10pm-3am Thu-Sat; Ⓜ Porta Romana

From the Klaxons and Babyshambles to REM and the Violent

HAVE TICKET, WILL TRAVEL

With the exception of international acts that take the stage at Magazzini Generali or Rolling Stone, most bands actually play venues outside the city. When you get your tickets, check the details for specially organised shuttle buses to and from the show. Otherwise, this is how to reach the major stadium-band venues:

FilaForum (☎ 02 488571; www.filaforum.it; Via di Vittorio, Agasso; Ⓜ Romolo/Famagosto, then shuttle bus)

Largo Idroscalo (Circolo Magnolia; 🚌 73, StarFly shuttle from Stazione Centrale to Linate Airport)

PalaVobis & Mazda Palace (☎ 02 334 00 551; Viale Sant'Elia 33; Ⓜ Lampugnano)

San Siro Stadium (Via Piccolomini; Ⓜ Lotto)

Villa Arconati (☎ 02 350 05 501; Castellazzo di Bollate; 🚌 Cadorna to Bollate Nord, then shuttle bus)

Femmes, they've all played Milan's leading rock venue. Patrons have been known to shower bands with adoration or contempt (ie beer) from the bar above the stage, but be warned, management keeps a lookout for amp-destroying rabble-rousers.

⭐ SURFER'S DEN
Club, Live venue

☎ 02 910 13 519, 02 545 6760; Via Mantova 13; Ⓜ Lodi

Milan's only surf club, with higgledy-piggledy longboards lining the walls, is admittedly a long way from the nearest break, but gets the idea of a good night out. In this case it's excellent DJs, the odd live performance and people who like to stay up late and dance.

◾ TEATRO CARCANO *Theatre*
☎ 02 5518 1377; www.teatrocarcano .com; Corso di Porta Romana 63; Ⓜ Crocetta

Many of the greats of Italian drama have trod the boards of this historic early 19th-century theatre. Now it hosts a solid programme of rep and new productions in Italian.

>NAVIGLI, PORTA TICINESE & ZONA TORTONA

South of the Duomo, the chain shops of Via Torino gradually morph into the city's hippest shopping strip, Corso di Porta Ticinese. Streetwear retailers and bars scream 'youthquake' against remnants of Milan's ancient past. Parco delle Basiliche links San Lorenzo to the Darsèna, the artificial lake that marks the beginning of Navigli. Milan was once defined by its network of canals, though as recently as the early '90s, after a long decline, the area was considered dangerous. Today it's known for dining and nightlife, with a slew of interesting shops and the city's best antiques market. To the west, over Graffitti Bridge from Porta Genova, is Zona Tortona, a once working-class tangle of tenements and factories, now flush with shopkeepers, ateliers and design companies. This is also home to the head offices of Diesel and Armani (look for the Tadao Ando–designed Armani Teatro on Via Bergognone). During the annual Salone del Mobile in April, Zona Tortona hosts satellite shows, launches and parties – a destination in itself.

NAVIGLI, PORTA TICINESE & ZONA TORTONA

☉ SEE
Design Library **1** B2
Fondazione Arnaldo
  Pomodoro..................**2** A2
San Lorenzo Columns.....**3** E1
San Lorenzo Maggiore ...**4** E1

☐ SHOP
American Apparel **5** E1
Antonioli **6** C3
Biffi............................**7** D1
Brazilian......................**8** E1
Casa di Minea **9** B2
Elizabeth the First........**10** E1
Frip **11** E1
Frippino **12** E1
i-Milano Tortona **13** C2

Mauro Bolognesi..........**14** C3
Nana's Thrift Store **15** B2

☷ EAT
Acquasala **16** C3
Al Pont de Ferr............**17** C3
Bussarakham...............**18** C3
Café Romeo Gigli **19** C3
Cantina della Vetra **20** E1
Design Library Café ......(see 1)
El Brellin **21** D3
Gelateria Le Colonne **22** E1
La Cozz.......................**23** A2
Le Vigne **24** C3
Piquenique **25** B2
Pizzeria del Ticinese.....**26** E1
Riva Reno **27** E3
Shri Ganesh **28** B4

☷ DRINK
Bigne **29** B2
Boccino......................(see 29)
Café PortNoy **30** E1
Capetown Café **31** D2
Le Biciclette................**32** D1
Le Coquetel **33** E2

★ PLAY
Auditorium di Milano....**34** D4
Boat Tours **35** D3
Bond.........................**36** C3
Cinema Mexico............**37** A2
Scimmie......................**38** D4
Shu **39** E1

NAVIGLI, PORTA TICINESE & ZONA TORTONA

👁 SEE

👁 DESIGN LIBRARY

☎ 02 894 21 225; www.designlibrary.it; Via Savona 11; yearly membership €25; ⏰ 10am-6.30pm Mon-Tue & Fri, 10am-4.30pm Wed, 10am-5pm Sat; Ⓜ Sant' Agostino

A design buff's dream: a white room lined with back issues of design bibles *Domus*, *Abitare* and *Ottogono*; Phaidon design monographs; company catalogues and more.

👁 FONDAZIONE ARNALDO POMODORO

☎ 02 890 75 394; www.fondazione arnaldopomodoro.it; Via Andrea Solari 35; ⏰ 11am-6pm Wed-Thu, Sat & Sun, 11am-10pm Fri (last entry 1hr before closing); Ⓜ Sant' Agostino

Metal-loving Arnaldo Pomodoro's large-scale, sci-fi–tinged work is on show at this vast postindustrial space, but he also launched the foundation to highlight the work of upcoming sculptors.

👁 SAN LORENZO COLUMNS

Corso di Porta Ticinese; 🚊 Missori

The freestanding row of 16 Corinthian columns from Milan's Mediolanum heyday were salvaged from a crumbling Roman residence and lined up here to form the portico of the new church (right). Their pagan

spirit lingers; welcome to the site of many an evening's beery indulgence.

👁 SAN LORENZO MAGGIORE

Corso di Porta Ticinese 39; ⏰ 7.30am-12.30pm, 2.30-6.45pm; 🚊 Missori

The touching simplicity of this early Christian basilica with its central dome and squat towers managed to survive a substantial reconstruction in the 16th century. The octagonal *Cappella di Sant'Aquilino's* 4th-century mosaic of a toga-clad Jesus holding court is also the real deal; the highly individual and seemingly cosmopolitan apostles in his thrall make the millennia fly by.

🛍 SHOP

🛍 AMERICAN APPAREL

Fashion

☎ 02 581 04 455; www.americanapparel .net; Corso di Porta Ticinese 22; ⏰ 11am-8pm Mon-Sat; 🚊 3

Yes, they are big, bad and from downtown LA, but sometimes you really just need a teal hoodie in a hurry and don't want to traipse the whole of Milan and hope. We're just sayin'…

🛍 ANTONIOLI

Fashion, Menswear

☎ 02 365 66 494; www.antoniolishop .com; Via Paoli 1; ⏰ 3-7.30pm Mon, 11am-7.30pm Tue-Sun; Ⓜ Porta Genova

SAN SIRO

Officially it's called Stadio Giuseppe Meazza, after a Milanese champion of the 1930s and '40s, but to football fans it's simply San Siro. Milan's two football teams AC Milan and FC Internazionale (Inter) play here every weekend from October to May. The distinctive red-girdered roof and striped concrete towers were added when the stadium was renovated for the 1990 World Cup, the design also boosting its capacity to 85,700. Serie A fans head for the **Museo Inter e Milan** (☎ 02 404 2432; www.sansirotour.com; Via Piccolomini 5, Gate 21; admission €7/5; ⏰ 10am-5pm; Ⓜ De Angeli, then 🚌 16 or shuttle), boasting nonstop screenings of matches, memorabilia and trophies galore. Carnival-style papier-mâché dummies of two-dozen football stars (spot your favourite: Gullit, Rijkaard and Matthaus are all there) add a little light, if slightly surreal, relief. The accompanying stadium tour covers the locker room, where you can gingerly rest your bum on the same bench as countless naked football legends. (The museum closes 30 minutes before kick off-on match days, so don't get any ideas.)

Against the backdrop of this gutted former cinema, Antonioli's brainy Belgian line-up (Ann Demeulemeester, Dries Van Noten, Martin Margiela et al) looks even more intelligent than usual. The store carries both men's and women's ranges. Look out for the well-priced Humanoid knits.

🅰 BIFFI *Fashion*
☎ 02 831 1601; www.biffi.com; **Corso Genova 5 & 6;** ⏰ 3-7.30pm Mon, 9.30am-1.30pm & 3-7.30pm Tue-Sat; 🚋 2
Retailer Rosy Biffi spotted potential in the young Gio and Gianni long before Armani and Versace became household names (more recently, she got Milanese women hooked onto US cult-brand jeans). She has a knack for interpreting edgier trends and making them work for conformist Milan; check out her selection of international

fashion heavyweights for both men and women.

🅰 BRAZILIAN *Fashion*
☎ 02 832 41 997; **Corso di Porta Ticinese 24;** ⏰ 10.30am-8pm Tue-Sat, 3.30-8pm Mon; 🚋 3
More new-world shapes and colours in front of the columns, this time from south of the equator. Latin labels that the Milanese are learning to love include Osklen and Iodice.

🅰 CASA DI MINEA *Jewellery*
☎ 02 581 08 662; www.casadiminea .com; **Via Savona 17;** Ⓜ **Porta Genova**
Young Finnish designers use wood, resin, silk and brass to create intriguing and wearable pieces that sit somewhere between jewellery and accessories. Collections are seasonal.

🏠 ELIZABETH THE FIRST
Vintage

☎ 02 999 5886; www.elizabethe
first.com; Alzaia Naviglio Grande 44;
⏱ 11am-8pm Tue-Sun;
Ⓜ Porta Genova

As the Virgin Queen herself once said, the past cannot be cured; neither can a vintage frock obsession, especially when face to face with Pucci shifts and Gucci shirts, and plenty of other great '50s to '70s finds. The 'ethnic vintage' range – so very Mick and Marianne – includes Uzbekistani ikat print coats and embroidered Yunan jackets.

🏠 FRIP *Fashion, Music*

☎ 02 832 1360; www.frip.it; Corso di Porta Ticinese 16; ⏱ 3-7.30pm Mon, 11am-2pm & 3.30-7.30pm Tue-Sat; 🚇 3
A husband-and-wife, DJ-stylist duo highlight some of Milan's most avant-garde looks and sounds. Look for Azumi & David boot bags and strap-on gaffer tape jewels or Nakkna's divine draped jersey from Sweden; then head straight for the vinyl and CDs.

🏠 FRIPPINO *Children's wear*

☎ 02 365 07 451; Via Urbano III 3; ⏱ 3-7pm Mon, 10.30am-7pm Tue-Sat; 🚇 3
None of those John-John pan-collared pea coats or prim smocks here. It's rock 'n' roll preschool with striped T-shirts and skinny jeans aplenty.

🏠 I-MILANO TORTONA
Fashion

☎ 02 894 22 722; Via Tortona 12;
⏱ 9.30am-10pm Mon-Fri, noon-10pm Sat; Ⓜ Porta Genova

The clothes here are all about kicking back and looking like you've not made any kind of effort (an unusual concept in Milan). Earthy tones and natural fabrics reign, paired with plastic jelly shoes or Bensimon plimsoles.

🏠 MAURO BOLOGNESI
Vintage, Antiques

☎ 02 837 6028; www.maurobolognesi
.com; Ripa di Porta Ticinese 47;
⏱ 9.30am-12.30pm & 3-7pm Tue-Sat;
Ⓜ Porta Genova

Midcentury shops are surprisingly thin on the ground in Milan (presumably because everyone was wise enough to hold onto their hand-me-down Arco lamps and Murano art glass). That makes this collection – Danimarca sideboards, white-on-white biomorphic vases, colour-blocked wall hangings and Kay Bojesen monkeys scampering up the walls – all the more special.

🏠 NANA'S THRIFT STORE
Fashion, Menswear

☎ 02 832 2770; Via Tortona 12;
⏱ 10am-9pm Mon-Fri, noon-8pm Sat;
Ⓜ Porta Genova

Ah, the labels that irrefutably prove the existence of hipster

Gentucca Bini
Fashion Designer, Romeo Gigli Creative Director

Most unexpected thing about Milan? Rigorous, austere avenues and 1940s Rationalist buildings hide enchanted gardens of the 16th century, cloisters of the 13th century and other artistic wonders. It's a complex and introspective city that constantly leaves you surprised. **Milan's best shopping?** I don't like shops that represent the choice of someone else; I like an object or a dress to attract my attention as I walk through the city, say at the fleamarket in Via Corsico or at G Lorenzi (**p67**) in the Quad. **Favourite building?** Studio BBPR's Torre Velasca (**p48**). **Best fashion people-watching?** Stazione Centrale (**p102**): it's a mirror of Milan's social complexity set against absolute architectural severity. **What is the colour of Milan?** White: the sum of all colours. **Best Milan experience?** Go to Galli (**p56**), the oldest confectionery shop in town, and eat marron glacés. Milan's style? Sober, intimate, complex.

culture in Milan are here (Slimfit's handpainted T-shirts for one). Watch out for the killer *kilomode* sales, where samples and special editions are sold for €40 per kilo.

 # EAT

ACQUASALA
Italian, Puglian €€

☎ 02 894 23 983; www.acquasala.it; **Ripa di Porta Ticinese 71;** ⏰ **closed Mon;** Ⓜ **Porta Genova**

Cucina povera, once the preserve of the poor, had a fashionable revival a few years back. The nostalgic Puglian dishes here fit the description: crisp, baked rice with mussels and potatoes; and *oreciette* (Puglian ear-shaped pasta) with *cime di rape* (broccoli greens) and *fave e cicoria* (a rich puree of broadbeans served with bitter chicory).

AL PONT DE FERR *Italian* €€

☎ 02 894 06 277; **Ripa di Porta Ticinese 55;** ⏰ **12.30-2.30pm & 8pm-1am Mon-Sun;** Ⓜ **Porta Genova**

Navigli's *osterie* (restaurants/bars) can often disappoint on the food front, but Al Pont de Ferr lifts the game. Its casual charm can make you wonder if the prices aren't tourist-inflated. Look again; you'll see attention to detail and interesting regional ingredients, such as rabbit stews, *fonduta piemontese* (fondue), purée of cardoons and *baccalà* (dried cod) on a soup of fennel.

BUSSARAKHAM *Thai* €€€

☎ 02 894 22 415; **Via Valenza 13;** ⏰ **noon-2.30pm & 7.30-11pm Thu-Sun, 7.30-11pm Mon-Wed;** Ⓜ **Porta Genova**

The tasty Thai menu doesn't venture far beyond standards, but the setting is fabulously authentic. Wooden handcrafted nooks, delicate ceramics, orchid-adorned tables and welcoming staff transport you to a Bangkok five-star.

CAFÉ ROMEO GIGLI
Cafe €€

☎ 02 832 1909; **Via Angelo Fumagalli 6;** ⏰ **7pm-1am Mon-Sat, Sun by appointment;** Ⓜ **Porta Genova**

A departure for the prince of peplum, this diner – bedecked with Driade furniture – has a definite future utopia edge, even if the coffee-scented mascarpone comes in a chocolate container rather than a feeding tube. They haven't skimped on Starck chairs nor the Ron Arad sofas; don't forget you're here to eat rather than plan your next redecoration.

CANTINA DELLA VETRA
Italian €€

☎ 02 894 03 843; www.cantinadella vetra.it; **Via Pio IV 3;** ⏰ **7.30-11.30pm Mon-Fri, noon-3pm & 7.30-11.30pm Sat & Sun;** 🚋 **2, 3, 14**

This country-style place with big windows overlooking the Piazza Vetra sports gingham tablecloths but otherwise underplays the rustic element. The *salumi* (mixed cured meat) platter includes a mortadella *tartufata*, *lardo* and a pancetta *coppata* as well as regional salami. It's known for its wine cellar as much as for the hearty regional staples, and books out most nights.

🍴 DESIGN LIBRARY CAFÉ
Italian   €€

☎ 02 894 23 329; Via Savona 11; ⏲ 7.30am-10.30pm Mon, 7.30am-11.30pm Tue-Thu, 7.30am-2am Fri, 5pm-2am Sat; Ⓜ Porta Genova

Lounge around on the window-side sofas, sit at the serpentine bar or get to work at one of the subtly lit tables (white MacBooks match nicely). Food here upholds the oldest design dictate in the book: KISS. Carpaccio of zucchini is served with a light lemon foam, risotto with the freshest white asparagus, and roast beef with rosemary potatoes.

🍴 EL BRELLIN *Italian*   €€€

☎ 02 581 01 351; www.brellin.com; cnr Vicolo dei Lavandai 14 & Alzaia Naviglio Grande 14; ⏲ 7pm-2am Mon-Sat; Ⓜ Porta Genova

Housed in a 1700s laundry, El Brellin's candlelit garden is a romantic

Lounge around at the Design Library Café

spot for made-on-the-premises pasta and classic Milanese specialties. The Sunday brunch buffet is laden with platters of cured meats, scrambled eggs, whole smoked salmon, and homemade desserts including the Milanese in-joke, biscuit-filled chocolate 'salami'. Come early to nab a table.

🍴 GELATERIA LE COLONNE
Gelateria   €

☎ 02 837 2292; Corso do Porta Ticinese 75; Ⓜ Missori

Artisan ice cream in wild flavours such as amaretto, orange blossom and *genepi* (an alpine herb) are served from this retro-styled and popular *gelateria*.

🍴 LA COZZ
Seafood, French €€

☎ 02 477 11 145; www.lacozz.it; Via Savona 41; ⏱ 10am-11.30pm Tue-Sun; Ⓜ Porta Genova

Moules et frites (mussels and fries) get a Milanese makeover in this rollicking temple to the mollusc. Have them done a number of pan-European ways, from cream and Pernod to rocket and saffron. *Fines de clairs* or Breton oysters come raw or gratined for starters while desserts bring you back to Via Savona for a lemon *gelati* or a cup of grappa-laced hot chocolate.

🍴 LE VIGNE *Italian* €€

☎ 02 837 5617; Ripa di Porta Ticinese 61; ⏱ noon-3pm & 7-11pm Mon-Sat; Ⓜ Porta Genova

Blindfold yourself and point at the menu, because that's the only way to choose among zucchini flowers stuffed with artisanal herbed ricotta, risotto with shrimp and nasturtium flowers, and a salad of octopus, artichoke and zucchini.

🍴 PIQUENIQUE
Italian, French €€

☎ 02 422 97 225; www.piquenique milano.it; Via Bergognone 24; ⏱ noon-2.30pm Mon, noon-2.30pm & 7-11.30pm Tue-Fri, 7-11.30pm Sat, 12.30-3.30pm Sun; Ⓜ Porta Genova; Ⓥ

With its large bar, semiopen kitchen, easy-going staff and rustic furniture, Piquenique feels like your new best friend's country house. Terrines or smoked fish platters, simple hearty meat dishes and interesting vegetarian options let the organic ingredients shine. The design crowd descends on Sunday for American-style pancake brunches.

🍴 PIZZERIA DEL TICINESE
Pizzeria €€

☎ 02 894 02 970; Corso Di Porta Ticinese 65; ⏱ lunch 12.30-3pm Sat, dinner 7pm-1am Mon-Sun; 🚊 3

Vaulted exposed brick ceilings, dark wood furniture and a central wood-fired oven make this a warm, cosy place for pizza and beer. Special pizzas made with fresh, organic ingredients make sure it's packed every night.

🍴 RIVA RENO *Gelateria* €

☎ 02 890 77 147; www.rivareno.com; Viale Col di Lana 8; ⏱ 4pm-midnight; 🚊 9, 29

The *gelati* at this bright Bolognian *gelateria* has a uniquely soft, smooth texture, and flavours are similarly innovative: praline and amaretti, toasted pine nuts, and saffron crème with burnt caramel sesame seeds. Can't choose? The persimmon sorbet is soothingly simple.

SADLER
Contemporary Italian €€€
☎ 02 581 04 451; www.sadler.it;
Via Ascanio Sforza 77; ⏱ 7.30-11.30pm
Mon-Sat; M Porta Genova
Get ready for a serious tummy-cramming session and Claudio Sadler's culinary wisdom: Sardinian *fregola* pasta with broad beans, pigeon ragout and cocoa, scabbard fish with borage-and-chickpea fritters or horse tartare, with crisped parmesan, peppers and fruity black truffles.

SHRI GANESH
Indian €€
☎ 02 581 10 933; www.shriganesh.it;
Via Elia Lombardini 8; ⏱ 7.30-11pm
Tue-Sun; M Porta Genova
Formally dressed staff can be either discreet or happy to chat, depending on *your* mood. Either way, they'll fill you up with a meat or vegetable thali that's complexly spiced and prettily presented, or ask them to bring on the banquet. There are tandoor dishes too.

DRINK

BIGNE *Bar, Gelateria*
☎ 02 581 09 986; cnr Via Tortona 21 &
Via Bugatti; M Porta Genova
This old-style wooden bar does nicely for a quick Campari or a *gelati* scooped from a metal-domed container (or a combination of the two). Big brother **Boccino** (☎ 02 894 15 562) next door is equally charming if you choose to linger.

CAFÉ PORTNOY *Bar*
☎ 02 581 13 429;
Corso di Porta Ticinese 10; 3
Wide windows and a corner position make this tiny bar seem expansive, as do the friendly bar staff, regulars and piled-on crostini come *aperitivo* time.

CAPETOWN CAFÉ *Bar*
☎ 02 894 03 053; Via Vigevano 3;
⏱ 7-2am; M Porta Genova
This straightup bar is where the locals come to down the best bloody marys and mojitos in Milan and hide from the weekend Navigli hordes.

LE BICICLETTE *Bar*
☎ 02 581 04 325; www.lebiciclette.com;
Via Torti 4; ⏱ 6pm-2am Mon-Sat &
12.30-2pm Sun; M Sant' Agostino
This one-time bike warehouse has done a complete giro-Italia to become one of the best *aperitivi* bars in Milan. A combination of luck and earliness will snag you a coveted low couch with glassed-in bicycle memorabilia underfoot, and first pick of the tasty dishes crowding the bar.

▼ LE COQUETEL *Bar*
☎ 02 836 0688; Via Vetere 14;
🕑 8-2am; 🚋 3

This large, lush cocktail bar packs in a young alternative crowd for its *aperitivo* spread and footpath carousing. There's free wi-fi, chilled South American bar staff and DJ nights.

PLAY

☆ AUDITORIUM DI MILANO
Concert hall
☎ 02 833 89 201; www.auditoriumdi milano.org; Largo Gustav Mahler, Corso San Gottardo 42a; 🕑 box office 10am-7pm; Ⓜ Porta Genova

Abandoned after WWII, the Cinema Massimo was transformed in 1999 into the state-of-the-art home to Milan's legendary Giuseppe Verde Symphonic Orchestra and Milan Chorus, as well as a venue for visiting international jazz acts and chamber music groups.

☆ BOND *Club*
☎ 02 581 08 375; Via Paoli 2;
🕑 10pm-3am Tue-Sun;
Ⓜ Porta Genova

A grunge-free late-nighter on the Naviglio Grande, owned by stylish retailer Claudio Antonioli.

☆ CINEMA MEXICO *Cinema*
☎ 02 489 51 802; www.cinemamexico.it; Via Savona 57; 🚋 14; Ⓜ Porta Genova

Don't be put off by its other name: Rocky Horror House. On Thursday the films are VO (version original), so you won't need a sweet t-t-trans-lator. Check the Sound & Motion section of the website for the quarterly programme.

☆ ROCKET *Live venue*
☎ 02 895 03 509; www.therocket.it; Via Pezzotti 52; 🚋 15

This cavelike venue hosts the odd live act along the lines of Glasgow's Futureheads. DJ nights vary; just know that you won't get the Eros Ramazzoti that's on the decks elsewhere. The whole operation ups sticks to beachside Sestri Levante during the summer; check the website for details.

THE BOATMAN'S CALL

Designer yachts and cruisers have become a fixture of the Salone del Mobile but you don't need to BYO to get out on the canals. Regular **boat tours** (☎ 02 667 9131 Mon-Fri, 02 332 27 336 Sat & Sun, Alzaia Naviglio Grande 4, at the Porta Genova area near the Scodellino bridge, €12) operate Friday and Saturday, and take in the historical canal-side laundries, dockyards and Conchetta lock.

Check out the big screen at Cinema Mexico

SCIMMIE *Live venue*
☎ 02 894 02 874; www.scimmie.it;
Via Cardinale Ascanio Sforza 49;
🕑 8pm-3am Mon-Sat;
Ⓜ Porta Genova

Jazz, alternative rock and blues are the stock in trade of the emerging talents who play to the overflowing crowds inside Scimmie, in the garden, and on its summertime jazz barge. Concerts start at 10pm, and the €8 to €15 admission fee includes your first drink.

SHU *Club, Bar*
☎ 02 583 15 720; www.shumilano.it;
cnr Via Molino delle Armi & Via della Chiusa; 🕑 6pm-2am nightly; Ⓜ Missori

The mothership has landed. Two monumental gold arms support a green ceiling with a matrix of circuitry that keeps you hoping George Clinton might just come and save you (from the commercial house, from yourself). Come early for *aperitivo* with a happy, unpretentious crowd or get ready to queue later on.

>CORSO MAGENTA, SANT'AMBROGIO & THE WEST

It's usually Leonardo da Vinci's *Cenacolo*, or the basilica of Sant'Ambrogio that draws visitors here, but there's an equal mix of the scared and the secular in these leafy streets. Claes Oldenburg's jutting *Needle, Thread and Knot* juts from the clamour of Cadorna Triennale station. Between here and the centre's Piazza Cordusio is the traditional home of high finance, and hence the *aperitivo* (aperitif) bars full of young bankers. To the south and the west, the watering holes grow more casual to cater to the students of the sprawling Università Cattolica del Sacro Cuore. There's talk that the Magenta neighbourhood is 'upcoming', but that's not to say it's in the process of gentrification. Always one of Milan's chicest, things have just become slightly less sedate, more accessibly stylish. Further west, you'll find the long-favoured shopping strip of the good *borghese*, Corso Vercelli. Furla, Mandarina Duck, Prenatal and Frette: almost every midrange Italian label is found here, as well as family-oriented *rosticcerie* (traditional take-away shops), pizzerias and, on Via Marghera, a clutch of packed *gelaterias*.

CORSO MAGENTA, SANT'AMBROGIO & THE WEST

◉ SEE

Basilica di Sant'Ambrogio.. 1　E3
Chiesa di San Francesco al
　　Fopponino .... 2　B3
Il Cenacolo
　　(The Last Supper)........... 3　D2
Museo Nazionale della
　　Scienza e della Tecnica.... 4　D3

▣ SHOP

Agua del Carmen................. 5　E3
Al Leone D'Oro..................... 6　E3
Amelia .... 7　E2
Buscemi Dischi .... 8　E2

E.Marinella .... 9　F2
Galleria Rossana Orlandi ... 10　C2
Henry Beguelin .... 11　E3
Il Mondo é Piccolo .... 12　D4
Nume............................... 13　F3
Pupi Solari .... 14　C1
Spazio Rossana Orlandi... 15　C2
Suede............................... 16　E3
To B................................. 17　D1

▥ EAT

Caffè Della Pusteria .... 18　E4
Chocolat .... 19　D1
Gelateria Marghera......... 20　A2

I Banchi Del Sole.............. 21　D1
Pane e Acqua.................... 22　C2
Pasticceria Cucchi............ 23　E4
Zero .... 24　C2

▼ DRINK

Bar Magenta...................... 25　E2
Noon................................. 26　D1
Noy .... 27　B2
Posteria De Amici .... 28　E3

★ PLAY

Habitus Culti Spa.............. 29　B2

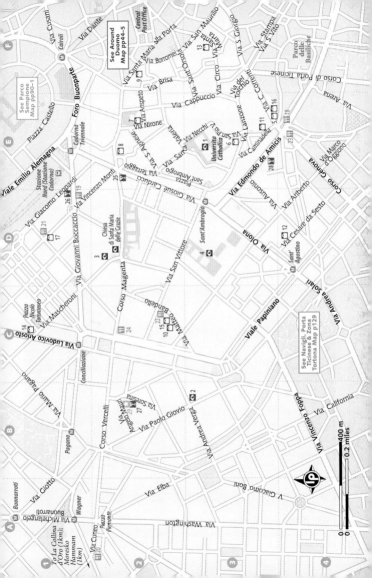

SEE

BASILICA DI SANT'AMBROGIO

☎ 02 864 50 895; Piazza Sant'Ambrogio 15; ⏱ basilica 7am-noon & 2-7pm Mon-Sat, 7am-1.15pm, 2.30-7.45pm Sun, museum 10am-noon & 3-5pm Mon, Wed-Fri, 3-5pm Sat & Sun; Ⓜ Sant'Ambrogio
St Ambrose, Milan's patron saint and one-time superstar bishop, is buried in the crypt of the mainly 11th-century Romanesque Basilica di Sant'Ambrogio, which he founded in AD 379. It's a fitting legacy, built and rebuilt with a purposeful simplicity that is truly uplifting: the seminal Lombard Romanesque basilica. Shimmering altar mosaics and a biographical AD 835 gilt altarpiece light up the shadowy vaulted interior. Along the south aisle, there's some precious 5th-century sparkle. Mosaics adorn the *Sacello San Vittore in Ciel d'Oro*, its 'golden sky' dome supported by winged monkeys and griffins.

CHIESA DI SAN FRANCESCO AL FOPPONINO

☎ 02 481 8049; Via Paolo Giovio 41; ⏱ 7.30am-noon & 3.30-7pm; Ⓜ Pagano

Marvel at the splendour of the Basilica di Sant'Ambrogio

PICOLO MILANO

With its urban, adult bustle and high proportion of grey days, Milan might not seem like a children-friendly destination. But there's plenty of pedestrianised streets for walking, piazzas for rest stops, and parks for running off all those sugary *brioche* breakfasts. Plus attractions that the local kids can't get enough of. Trains and bumper cars can be found in **Parco Sempione** (p92) and Piazza Gerusalemme playgrounds and there's an under-12s only park in the grounds of Villa Belgiojoso Bonaparte, the home of the **Galleria d'Arte Moderna** (p62). Corso Vercelli is where Milan's well-to-do families come to shop; you'll find kids clothes in all budget ranges. Choosing a new outfit and grabbing a *gelato* can make for a memorable Milanese afternoon. The rattling orange 29/30 tram is a kid-pleaser in itself, and circles the city's ancient gates; good for a game of historical make believe. Hop on at Piazza Repubblica, Viale Sturzo at the end of Corso Como, Corso Sempione or Porta Genova.

On rainy days make a beeline to:
> Castello Sforzesco (p89)
> Civico Acquario (p92)
> Museo Civico di Storia Naturale (p63)
> Museo Nazionale della Scienza e della Tecnica (☎ 02 485 551 200; www.museo scienza.org; Via San Vittore 21; admission €8/6; ☺ 9.30am-5pm Tue-Fri, 9.30am-6.30pm Sat & Sun; Ⓜ Sant'Ambrogio)
> Torre Branca (p94)

The 1964 Gio Ponti–designed church is out of the way but a must if you want to see the Milanese master's key works. The white facade's use of diamond motifs echoes the panes of a stained-glass window while Ponti's rendering of an archetypal church roofline evokes a child's elemental drawing.

🅒 IL CENACOLO (THE LAST SUPPER)
☎ 02 894 21 146; www.cenacolovinciano .it; Piazza Santa Maria delle Grazie 2, Corso Magenta; admission €6.50/free plus booking fee €1.50; ☺ 8.15am-6.45pm Tue-Sun by prior reservation only; Ⓜ Cadorna; ♿

Leonardo Da Vinci's famous **mural** is hidden away on one wall of the Cenacolo Vinciano, the refectory adjoining **Chiesa di Santa Maria delle Grazie**. His moving depiction of Christ and the disciples is one of the world's most iconic images (and was long before all the Dan Brown nonsense). Viewings are limited to groups of 25 for a strictly timed 15 minutes. You'll need to book anywhere from two weeks to three months in advance, although late cancellations, city tours and canny concierges can sometimes result in miraculous openings.

SHOP

AGUA DEL CARMEN
Fashion, Homewares

☎ 02 894 15 363; www.aguadel
carmen.it; Via Cesare Correnti 23;
🕑 3-7.30pm Mon, 10am-7.30pm Tue-Sat;
Ⓜ Sant'Ambrogio

Fornasetti faces appear to signal their approval of the great mix of ultrawearable clothes, shoes and bags. Orla Kiely totes, Pedro Garcia flats and Sylvie Quartara flip-flops are sensible (and sensibly priced) but have eye candy appeal too.

AL LEONE D'ORO *Antiques*

☎ 02 809480; Via Lanzone 16;
🕑 10.30am-1.30pm & 3-7pm Tue-Sat;
Ⓜ Sant'Ambrogio

The medieval streets around Sant'Ambrogio yield a host of surprises, not least this antique shop with a spectacular collection of paintings, and jewellery from the 1930s to 1950s.

AMELIA *Children's wear*

☎ 02 454 95 663; www.ameliamilano.it;
Via Ansperto 10; 🕑 10am-1pm & 3-7pm
Tue-Sat; Ⓜ Cadorna

Designer Katrin Arens' background in recycled interiors is reflected in her combination of classic shapes, simple hand-stitched decoration and attention to the tactile quality of fabrics. Clothes cut from the softest hemp, jersey, voile, pure wool and cotton feel as divine against the skin as they look. For babies and older children.

BUSCEMI DISCHI *Music*

☎ 02 804103; www.buscemi.com;
Corso Magenta 31; 🕑 3-7.30pm Mon,
9.30am-2pm & 3-7.30pm Tue-Sat;
Ⓜ Cadorna

We all go to Milan in search of a Jazzie B presents School Days CD, don't we? This is probably the only place in Milan to find it. Or get the classical desk's witheringly spot-on appraisal of the el-cheapo recording of Arvo Pärt you thought might make diverting hotel listening. It's been here since 1965, and downloads or no, it's here to stay.

E. MARINELLA
Fashion, Men's Wear

☎ 02 864 67 036; www.marinellanapoli
.it; Via Santa Maria Alla Porta 5; 🕑 3-
7.30pm Mon, 10am-7.30pm Tue-Sat;
Ⓜ Cairoli

Looking for something to go with the John Lobbs? Naples' legendary *su misura* (bespoke) tie-maker has finally made it to Milan. Heavy wooden drawers are filled with RTW silk beauties, subtly adorned with tiny flowers or geometric patterns. Once inside this elegant, private atelier though, you'll be sure to want a precisely fitted six-fold wool-lined fat-knot number. Their advice: 'the *only* rule is to follow the instinct'.

🏠 GALLERIA ROSSANA ORLANDI *Fashion*
☎ 02 467 4471; www.galleriarossana orlandi.com; Via Matteo Bandello 16; ☽ 10am-7pm Tue-Sat; Ⓜ Conciliazione
Super stylist Rossana Orlandi's fashion choices are no less inspired than her interiors. Clothes here depart from the OTT Milanese norm with some pieces paired back, smart and pretty, others totally left of field. Dare we say it feels a little French?

🏠 HENRY BEGUELIN *Fashion*
☎ 02 720 00 959; Via Caminadella 7; ☽ 3-7.30pm Mon, 10.30am-7.30pm Tue-Sun Ⓜ Sant'Ambrogio
Softly unconstructed coats, strappy sandals and earthily decorated bags are handmade using leather that's been tanned and dyed using traditional techniques. The haute-hippy look is also carried through to linen separates for summer.

🏠 IL MONDO É PICCOLO *Toys*
☎ 02 581 06 086; Via Cesare da Sesto 19; Ⓜ Sant'Agostino
These imaginative, well-crafted toys are just the ticket to amuse

DESIGNER OUTLETS
There's no lack of discount shopping in Milan but for real range and variety, plan a trip to the outlet malls. Most large Italian labels and many global brands are represented; discounts range from the pallid to the pulse-quickening. See the following reviews for transport options or check the individual websites for driving instructions.

Fox Town (☎ 091 630 08 03; www.foxtown.ch; Via A. Maspoli 18, Mendrisio, Switzerland; ☽ 11am-7pm) is 50km north of Milan in Switzerland, and has over 160 shops that run the gauntlet from Feragamo to Nike in a multilevel mall. There's a coach service for shoppers or catch a Switzerland-bound train to Chiasso then Swiss Postbus to the mall.

Serravalle Scrivia (☎ 0143 609000; www.mcarthurglen.it/serravalle; Via della Moda, 1, Serravalle Scrivia; ☽ 10am-8pm) is around 80km south of Milan on the way to Genoa. This Ligurian version of an outdoor SoCal-style mall, has faux two-storied streets and over 180 shops, including Frette, Dolce & Gabbana and Petite Bateau. The same coach company that services Fox Town also does Serravalle (return €15; www.zaniviaggi.it), or catch a local Milan–Genoa train to Arquata Scrivia.

The Place (☎ 015 249 6199; www.theplaceoutlet.com; Strada Trossi, Sandigliano; ☽ 3-7pm Mon, 10am-7pm Tue-Sat, 11am-7pm Sun) is halfway between Milan and Turin. Billed as a 'luxury outlet', the Ermenegildo Zegna group has gathered upmarket Italian brands like Gucci, La Perla and Bellora together in a 'village' in view of the Alps. There's no direct public-transport link; a change of trains and a taxi from the station is required.

CORSO MAGENTA, SANT'AMBROGIO & THE WEST

young minds and cater to second childhoods. It's never too late to enjoy a wheeled wooden duck on a stick.

NUME *Design, Children's wear*
☎ 02 805 2838; www.nume-design.it; Via Santa Marta 14; ☼ 10am-1.30pm & 3-7pm Tue-Sat; Ⓜ Missori
Hand-stitched felt pillows that declare '*stella stellina, la notte si avvicina*' (little star, the night is coming), a long-time favourite Italian lullaby, pair beautifully with simply designed kids furniture at this individual children's design shop. Search out the interlocking cardboard construction sets, which are kid-pleasing and very stylish too.

PUPI SOLARI
Children's Wear, Fashion
☎ 02 463325; Piazza Tommaseo 2; ☼ 10am-7.30pm Tue-Sat; Ⓜ Conciliazione 🚊 29, 30
Many Milanese from a certain kind of family will recall regular Pupi Solari visits for shoe fittings and picking out exquisitely decorated party dresses or tweed jackets just like daddy's. The wonderfully lavish window displays still delight; there's now a women's department and in the same square, a men's-wear branch Host.

SPAZIO ROSSANA ORLANDI
Homewares
☎ 02 467 4471; www.rossanaorlandi.com; Via Matteo Bandello 14; ☼ 10am-7pm Tue-Sat; Ⓜ Conciliazione
The path to this iconic interior's *spazio* can seem like a Jungian quest: innocently ring, ring that bell, wonder if the second gate will ever open, then find yourself adrift in an interiors mag photoshoot, next in an office gormlessly peering at an inspiration board for clues. When you do find the shop (it's up the mysterious back stairs), a dreamlike treasure trove of quite out-of-the-ordinary objects and homewares, stacked on ink-stained shelves, awaits your exploration.

SUEDE *Fashion*
☎ 02 581 18 308; Via Cesare Correnti 21; ☼ 3-7.30pm Mon, 10.30am-7.30pm Tue-Sun; Ⓜ Sant'Ambrogio
A rare chance to fill out your wardrobe with fun directional dresses and separates at rock-bottom prices (without the hovering panic attack of the Zara or H&M change rooms). Shoes don't skimp on style either and come in rainbow shades.

TO B *Fashion*
☎ 02 480 24 947; Via Vincenzo Monti 27; ☼ 3-7.30pm Mon, 10am-7.30pm Tue-Sat; Ⓜ Cadorna

Here's a well-chosen range of T-shirts and casual wear that fills a packing gap in a flash. Bensimon plimsoles and espridrilles come in myriad colours for similar coordination quick-fixes.

EAT

CAFFÈ DELLA PUSTERLA
Cafe €

☎ 02 894 02 146; Via Edmondo de Amicis 24; ⏰ 7-2am Mon-Sat, 9-2am Sun, kitchen from 10am; Ⓜ Sant'Ambrogio

This rambling woody bar pulls a student crowd night and day but is most famed for its fabulous range of filled breakfast *cornettos* (croissants) and stash of international magazines and newspapers. At 8am the pistachio-filled variety can startle the sleepy with a spurt of sci-fi green ooze but are finger-licking good regardless.

CHOCOLAT
Gelateria, Cafe €€

☎ 02 481 05 597; www.chocolatmilano .it; Via Boccaccio 9; ⏰ 7.30-1am; Ⓜ Cadorna

As this slick-interiored *gelateria's* name suggests, it plays flavour favourites. Variations on the chocolate theme include milk, dark, white, chilli, *gianduja* (chocolate-hazelnut) and cinnamon. People have been known to eat a crusty smoked salmon *panini* or a slice of fragrant home-baked almond

cake here, but the crowds that queue out on the road come for the cups and cones.

GELATERIA MARGHERA
Gelateria €

☎ 02 468641; Via Marghera 33; Ⓜ De Angeli

Concerted queuing is often required at this famous *gelateria*.

WORTH A TRIP: D'O

When you've got a Michelin-starred restaurant and a cool, young Marchesi-trained chef-owner who charges a paltry €11.50 for a 2-course lunch, there has to be a catch, right? Well, there are two: **D'o** (☎ 02 936 2209; Via Magenta 18, San Pietro all'Olmo, Cornaredo; 2-course lunch €11.50, 4-course dinner €35 per person, incl water & coffee, cards not accepted; ⏰ noon-3pm & 7-10pm Tue-Sat) is in a small suburban village around 12km from the centre, and the restaurant has been known to be booked out four months in advance. But it's worth it. Davide Oldani's cooking is an ode to 'poor' ingredients and simplicity, his aim, to serve 'humble food made noble by technique' cheaply. Dishes might include tripe three ways, his signature caramelised onion tart with a parmesan sorbet and a warm parmesan sauce or risotto with Jerusalem artichokes and vanilla. It's around 25 to 40 minutes from Milan by car, not far from the Rho Fiera, or possible via metro to Molino Dorino then a taxi.

Its range of ice-cream cakes and *liquorini* – layered *gelati* or sorbet with fruit or nut toppings and, you guessed it, liquor – are worth the wait.

🍴 IL GIRASOLE
Health Food   €€
☎ 02 896 97 459; Via Vincenzo Monti 32; ⏰ 10am-7pm Tue-Sat; Ⓜ Cadorna
You'll find a wide assortment of specialist health food and natural products in this cheerful corner shop. Gluten-free and whole-grain versions of Italian staples are a good find for those with allergies or overwhelmed by the 24/7 white-flour deluge. There's skincare, organic fresh produce and artisan rennet-free cheeses. Next door, there is an upmarket vegetarian restaurant.

🍴 LA COLLINA D'ORO
Japanese, Chinese,
Southeast Asian   €€
☎ 02 404 3148; Via Rubens 24; ⏰ 11am-3pm & 6.30-11.30pm Tue-Sun; Ⓜ De Angeli
A bright modern interior by the studio of Radical design-guru Alessandro Mendini sets the scene for a pan-Asian menu that includes Chinese and Japanese staples but also, unusually for Milan, some Southeast Asian dishes. A bustling local favourite.

🍴 PANE E ACQUA
Contemporary Italian   €€€
☎ 02 481 98 622; www.paneacqua.com; Via Matteo Bandello 14; ⏰ 7.30-11pm Mon, 9am-11pm Tue-Sat; Ⓜ Conciliazione
Super-stylist Rossana Orlandi has transformed a former corner *tabacchi* (corner shop) into Milan's most original and intriguing restaurant. Stark oversized clocks and raw concrete walls are softened by terrazzo floors and an ever-changing explosion of seasonal colour and texture. (For spring, shocking pink blowsy roses decorate the bar, and farmhouse chairs are painted to match.) The food is complex but never modish: a basil-scented cereal and seafood soup is served in steep-sided beaten pewter bowls, hand-cut spaghetti with *baccalà* (dried cod) and Taggiasche olives is laced with a rich, briny stock. Desserts are equally simple and spot-on: a rich splodge of buffalo ricotta is daubed with dark caramel and strewn with bitter chocolate nibs. Service is both kindly and unusually knowledgeable.

🍴 PASTICCERIA CUCCHI
Pasticceria   €
☎ 02 894 09 793; Corso Génova 1; ⏰ 10am-8pm Tue-Sun; Ⓜ Sant'Ambrogio
One of Milan's most beautiful old-school *pasticcerias* (cake shops),

Cucchi is set in a peaceful neighbourhood square. Snaffle a *brioche* at the bar or slowly disassemble a *bundino di riso* (a cylindrical tart filled with rice pudding) under the trees outside or the chandelier in the back room.

ZERO *Contemporary Japanese, Crudo* €€€
☎ 02 454 74 733; www.zeromagenta.it; **Corso Magenta 87;** ☽ **restaurant 7.30pm-midnight Mon-Sat, shop 12.30-2.30pm Tue-Sat;** Ⓜ **Conciliazione**
Is this the ultimate in Milan-style Japanese dining? The dramatically designed space puts the spotlight on the kitchen which prepares traditional sashimi but also a variety of creative raw and rare dishes. Japanese technique dominates, while the menu flirts with Italian flavours and ingredients (including a *carpaccio*-style Angus beef). Meanwhile, *shōchū* cocktails appear to be the new *negroni*. Bookings are hard to come by; if you miss out, opt for some stylishly got-up takeaway.

DRINK

BAR MAGENTA *Bar*
☎ 02 805 3808; www.barmagenta100 .com; Via Giosué Carducci 13; ☽ daily; Ⓜ Cadorna
Grab a seat in this historic bar and let Milan come to you. Drift in during the day for espresso,

sandwiches and beer, or join the students during early evening for wine from a tap and a pavement position under the Liberty signage.

NOON *Bar*
☎ 02 480 24 607; www.noonmilano.com; **Via Boccaccio 4;** ☽ **noon-2am;** Ⓜ **Cadorna**
The finance crowd spilling out onto the footpath terrace of NooN's big-windowed, corner bar don't hint at the sprawling proportions within. (Though the surreal number of scooters strewn about via Leopardi come nightfall might.) Upstairs, downstairs, and halfway in between, there's a cigar bar, basement club space and a large à la carte restaurant.

NOY *Bar*
☎ 02 481 10 375; www.noyweb.com; **Via Soresina 4;** ☽ **noon-2am Tue-Fri, 10-2am Sat, 10am-midnight Sun;** Ⓜ **Conciliazione**
With its uptight-housewife-gets-her-groove-back-at-the-ashram decor, only the corrugated roof gives this former garage's past life away. A poke at the fresh and generous *aperitivo* spread starts the night right. Cocktails, perfect for retoxing after a wellness treatment at Habits Culti (p150) next door, come next.

▼ POSTERIA DE AMICI *Bar*

☎ 02 832 42 358; Via Edmondo De Amicis 33; ⏰ noon-midnight; Ⓜ Sant'Ambrogio

Locals pack out this place for the wine, music and *tigelle Modenesi*, filled foccacia-like rolls, Modena-style. Eager to please staff and a lime-washed, country-style interior are welcoming.

★ PLAY

★ HABITS CULTI SPA *Spa*

☎ 02 485 17 588; www.habitsculti.it; Via Angelo Mauri 5; ⏰ 11am-10pm Mon-Sat, 10am-8pm Sun; Ⓜ Conciliazione

Culti's ethno-sacred aesthetic lives large at this seriously sensual spa. The touted total well being, radiance and renewed internal resources don't come cheap (prices start at €80 for a basic manicure) but this is no corner nail bar. Stone, wood and water are highlighted in the decor and treatments take their cues from the same elements, as well as utilising flowers, salts and mud.

★ MORESKO HAMMAM *Spa*

☎ 02 404 6936; www.moresko.it; Via Rubens 19; ⏰ noon-11pm Mon, Wed & Thu, noon-midnight Sat, 10am-10pm Sun, bookings required; Ⓜ De Angeli

Through the courtyard and out the back of a nondescript apartment building, you'll find this lovingly run, friendly *hammam*. As well as a steam room, bathing facilities, massage and beauty treatments (including traditional sugar hair removal), you can relax in the peaceful lounge with mint tea and *lokum* (Turkish delight) or an *aperitivo*. Check for single-sex opening hours and bathing suit requirements.

>EXCURSIONS

Enjoy the breathtaking views and fresh air in Bergamo Alta (p152)

EXCURSIONS

BERGAMO

There's no shortage of urban appeal in this eastern Lombard town, but there's also fresh air, breathtaking views and, in Bergamo Alta, few cars.

Although within commuting distance from Milan, Bergamo has always been staunchly independent, spending much of its history as a Venetian city-state and the supremely elegant, discreetly wealthy Bergamaschi still display a charming self-possession.

The city's defining feature is a double identity. The ancient hilltop *città alta* (upper town), is a tangle of tiny medieval streets, embraced by 5km of Venetian walls. The main street is full of well-stocked *enoteche* (restaurants) and *alimentari* (grocery store and deli) as well as gems like **Daniela Gregis** (☎ 035 236833; via Gombito 2), who stocks her own clothing line as well as Catiglioni stools and ballet slippers of magenta satin. There's enticing *pasticceria* (cake shops) too; skip the signature *polenta e osei*, a sickly sweet tromp l'oeil polenta and songbird pie, and opt for a *lingue di gatti* (cat's tongue) or *baci di dama* (lady's kiss). Restaurants serve rabbit, pork-stuffed ravioli, and creamy polenta or buckwheat with everything.

Connected by a funicular, sprawling *città bassa* (lower town) is not as unlovely as reported. Its streets of *palazzi* (palaces) and buildings from the early 20th century to the '60s are intriguing, plus there's great shopping.

Sadly the Renaissance paintings that line the Accademia Carrara won't be seen again until 2010, while it's being restored. Across the road, however, **Galleria d'Arte Moderna e Contemporanea** (GAMeC; ☎ 035 270272; www.gamec .it; Via San Tomaso 53; €4/2.50; ☀ 10am-7pm Tue-Sun, to 10pm Fri) has a permanent collection of 20th-century work including that of Lucio Fontana, Giorgio Morandi and Victor Pasmore, and excellently curated contemporary shows.

INFORMATION

Location 40km east of Milan

Getting there There are almost-hourly trains from Stazione Centrale (www.ferroviedel lostato.it; €4.10/2.05, 50 minutes); ATB's bus 1 connects the train station with the funicular to the upper city, though walking is an option too.

Information www.apt.bergamo.it

When to go Weekends can get crowded with both Milanese and short haul travellers, though not unbearably so; like Milan, many shops and restaurants close in August.

BELLAGIO

It's impossible not to be smitten by Bellagio's waterfront of bobbing boats, its rugged, zigzagging streets, red-roofed buildings, dark cypress groves and rhododendron-filled gardens. Unfortunately, on a sunny spring or summer Sunday most of Milan and a good swag of international travellers will be sharing in the enchantment. The noise, clamour and queues can really ruin what could be a beautiful friendship. Weekdays in the low season are a different matter when its blissfully quiet and touchingly melancholy, and often a good few degrees warmer than Milan.

You can get up close and personal with the entire town in an hour or two, leaving you with blessedly little to do other than enjoy a leisurely lunch, wander aimlessly, while away the afternoon with a bottle of the local Mamete Prevostini Opera Bianco in a vaulted-roofed cafe, or hop the slow boat back to Como. Twelfth-century San Giacomo has lost none of its Lombard high Romanesque charms, and you can also explore two of Bellagio's splendid villas: **Villa Serbelloni** (☺ garden tours only 11am & 4pm Tue-Sun; €6.50/3, limited tickets sold 10 minutes in advance) and **Villa Melzi** (☎ 03 195 1281; €5/3; ☺ 9am-6pm Mar-Oct) with its magnificent gardens and Egyptian art collection. Silk and handcraft shops abound but are for the most blandly similar and comically overpriced. Como is a slightly better option for flashing the credit card. Tip: if you've purchased a return ticket for the ferry or hydrofoil, you still need to book your place on a returning boat; this is best done on arrival in peak period as they fill up fast.

INFORMATION
Location 75km north of Milan
Getting there Trains depart hourly from Milan's Cadorna station to the lakeside Como Nord Lago (www.lenord.it; €3.50/1.75, one hour) or take the Switzerland-bound Cisalpino from Stazione Centrale to Stazione San Giovanni (www.ferroviedellostato.it; €6.50/5.50; 40 minutes) although it's less convenient for ferries. From the jetty, take an hourly hydrofoil (45 minutes), bus (75 minutes) or scenic ferry (two hours) to Bellagio.
Information www.bellagiolakecomo.com
When to go The lake certainly sparkles in summer but ferries and the town itself can be hellishly crowded; September to April is a different story.

VERONA

Plenty of places claim to be for lovers, but Verona takes its role seriously. The fugues and feuds of the Scaligeri, the city's 14th-century rulers, were legend, and inspired a string of poets not least of all William Shakespeare. Only the curmudgeonly will question if tortured teens Romeo and Juliet existed. It's Juliet's town, after all. Visit her house, complete with a much-pledged-beneath balcony, **Casa di Giulietta** (☎ 045 803 43 03; Via Cappello 23; €4/1; 8.30am-7.30pm Tue-Sun, 1.45-7.30pm Mon) or San Zeno Maggiore, the church where the couple's clandestine union was supposedly consecrated. It's also one of Italy's most splendid Romanesque basilica, with Mantegna's winsome and distracted Madonna richly framed as an altarpiece and walls festooned with equally remarkable 12th-century frescoes.

Verona itself is an architectural aphrodisiac, with fairy-tale palazzos of striped brick and marble and narrow, secretive streets. Take in the 360-degree Renaissance charm of Piazza delle Erbe, or head to Scaligeri Palazzo to pay your respects to Dante, the poet who braved the inferno for his Beatrice and found peace here. The drama doesn't stop there. Opera is staged in the 1st-century AD Roman amphitheatre on balmy summers nights; when 15,000 music lovers light their candles at sunset, wait for the goosebumps if not tears. All that emotion can leave you peckish and in need of a drink. Sip a *soave* (local dry white wine) and nibble on **L'Oste Scuro's** (☎ 45 592650; Vicolo San Silvestro 10) exquisite seafood *crudo* and whole fish baked in salt or meander through a plate of *bresaola* (aged air-dried beef), salamis, horse and prosciutto at one of the towns many wine bars.

INFORMATION

Location 160km east of Milan
Getting there Dozens of trains depart daily from Milan's Stazione Centrale to Verona's Porta Nuova (www.ferroviedellostato.it; €12.50/6.50, one hour 35 minutes). From station, take bus 11, 12, 13, 14, 72 or 73 to centre.
Information portale.comune.verona.it
When to go Is there a limit to your love?

LAGO MAGGIORE

Lago Maggiore might not boast rock-star residents and a Clooney-like Lake Como but its southern town of Stresa has pulled a few artists and writers in its time. Hemingway, who arrived in 1918 to tend his battle scars, was one. Scenes in *A Farewell to Arms* are set at the Grand Hotel des Iles Borromees, one of the most palatial of the hotels garlanding the lake. Stresa still has something of the belle-époque about it, both its lakeside promenade and cobbled old town.

This pretty Piedmontese western shore is sprinkled with picturesque villages and circled with palms and cypresses. But the deep blue lake's most dazzling attraction is, undoubtedly, the Borromean Islands. Isola Bella was named for the *bella* Isabella, first-lady of its 17th-century centre-piece, **Palazzo Borromeo** (☎ 03 233 0556; www.borromeoturismo.it; €11/5; ☼ 9am-5.30pm Mar-Oct). Presiding over 10 tiers of terraced gardens, the baroque palace is decorated with Tiepolo paintings and sculptures by Canova. Guests have included Napoleon and Josephine in 1797, and another ill-fated couple, Charles and Diana in 1985. What's left of the island swarms with *gelati*, pizza and souvenir stalls. The fabulous **Palazzo Madre** (☎ 03 233 0556; €10/5; ☼ 9am-5.30pm Mar-Oct) *is* the island of Madre, with white peacocks strutting waterfront gardens (sadly a 2006 tornado uprooted much of the island's historic botanica). Inside you'll find the Countess Borromeo's doll collection and a neoclassical puppet theatre care of a La Scala set designer, complete with a cast of devilish marionettes. Blissfully souvenir-stall free, the tiny island of Pescatori retains a fishing-village feel – what better spot for a lunch of grilled lake fish?

INFORMATION

Location 90km northwest of Milan
Getting there Stresa is on the Domodossola line from Milan and trains leave Milan's Stazione Centrale hourly (www.ferroviedellostato.it; €8.50/5.50, one hour).
Information www.illagomaggiore.com
When to go Weather is surprisingly mild year round; the islands all but close in winter.

>SNAPSHOTS

Milan's stellar reputation as a shopping destination precedes it, as does its status as happening design hub and its penchant for evening drinks. But it's also got surprises in store. Seek out a fabulously diverse culinary scene, vibrant live music venues and relatively undiscovered architectural and artistic gems.

> Accommodation   158
> Shopping   160
> Aperitivo   162
> Food   164
> Design   166
> Museums & Galleries   168
> Architecture   169
> Clubbing   170
> Music   171
> Fiera   172

Soak up the atmosphere among the jumbled outdoor tables at Frida (p108)

ACCOMMODATION

There are some memorable places to stay in Milan, from opulent old dames to slick new kids on the block. Dedicated hotel junkies, those on expense account junkets or big weekenders won't blink at the tariffs, but the rest of us might wonder if what's on offer justifies the big euros. Great value is difficult to come by in most budget ranges, and downright impossible during the Salone del Mobile, the fashion shows or other larger fairs. Many hotels charge for amenities you would take for granted elsewhere, including internet and basic continental breakfast. Wi-fi (or even the availability of a broadband cord) and bar fridges are never a given. That said, booking ahead and comparison-shopping online for 'special rates' can result in excellent deals, especially out of ultrapeak times. Always make sure you clarify any inclusions. The exceptions to the rule are delightful.

Don't forget to factor in location. The city's sprawl means what constitutes 'the centre' can be highly subjective. And confusingly, highly regarded hotels (like the Chedi and the Enterprise) are often located for easy access to the Fiera, but aren't convenient for short pleasure stays.

The cobbled streets surrounding the Duomo are brimming with hotels, large and small, luxurious and seen-better-days, and although premium priced and often overwhelmingly busy, make a lot of sense if you want to quickly take in the city on foot. Likewise, those in the Quadrilatero D'Oro, for those up to the challenge of the 24/7 style onslaught. Brera offers a more relaxed local feel without taking you too far out, as do the areas surrounding San Babila, the Giardini Pubblici and Corso Venezia. There are also a number of hotels at the Porta Garibaldi end of Corso Como; while excellent for shoppers and 24-hour party people, the area can be noisy – doof-doof-

Need a place to stay? Find and book it at lonelyplanet.com. Over 40 properties are featured for Milan – each personally visited, thoroughly reviewed and happily recommended by a Lonely Planet author. From hostels to high-end hotels, we've hunted out the places that will bring you unique and special experiences. Read independent reviews by authors and other travellers, and get practical information including amenities, maps and photos. Then reserve your room simply and securely via Hotels & Hostels – our online booking service. It's all at lonelyplanet.com/hotels.

doof – and the Garibaldi train, traffic and redevelopment vortex makes for a grim outlook from the multistorey places. Midrange and budget options cluster around the Stazione Centrale, and while the immediate vicinity is considered seedy at night, many places are also close to bustling Corso Buenos Aires and the nicely alternative scene around Lima. There are also midrange places in the streets running off Corso Sempione. These seem remote and put you out of easy reach of a metro stop, but the area is well serviced by Milan's charming trams, pleasantly residential and jam-packed with some of the best bars. Plus nearby Parco Sempione is a soothing spot for a stroll or morning run. The leafy streets around Corso Magenta and Corso Vercelli are also close to the park, have an upmarket appeal and are handy to the Malpensa Express. As one of Milan's main tourist draws, Navigli isn't blessed with hotels but this is changing with a few places springing up to appeal to the design crowd who descend upon Zona Tortona.

B&Bs and apartment rentals can be a stylish, spacious and slightly more affordable alternative to hotels, though again it's important to remember to double check the location, availability of amenities as well as photos and floorplans and be clear on price and booking conditions. You may also need to have a healthy sense of the absurd. If opting for apartment rentals, chains are not common and tend to be overpriced, so you'll most likely be dealing with Milanese landlords and housekeepers who can be a capricious lot. What seems too good to be true on a website often is.

BEST FOR OPULENCE

> Town House Galleria (www.town housegalleria.it)
> Four Seasons (www.fourseasons.com/milan)
> Park Hyatt Milan (www.milan.park.hyatt.com)
> Grand Hotel et de Milan (www.grand hoteletdemilan.it)
> Petit Palace (www.petitpalais.it)

BEST CONTEMPORARY BRIO

> Bulgari Hotel (www.bulgarihotels.com)
> The Gray (www.hotelthegray.com)
> The Straf (www.straf.it)
> The Nhow (www.nhow-hotels.com)

BEST SMALL & STYLISH

> 3 Rooms (www.3rooms-10corsocomo.com)
> Forestia Monforte (www.foresteria monforte.it)
> The Anderson (www.starhotels.com)
> Hotel Spadari al Duomo (www.spadari hotel.com)
> Hotel Manzoni (www.hotelmanzoni.com)

BEST FOR PEACE & QUIET

> Town House 12 (www.townhouse.it/th12)
> Town House 31 (www.townhouse.it/th31)
> Tara Verde (www.taraverde.it)
> Cesena 5 (www.cesena5.com)
> Vietnamour (www.vietnamonamour.com)

SHOPPING

Milan began to turn heads after WWII, when Italy's fashion industry boomed and rapidly outgrew the workshops of Florence. Today the heady rollcall of designers all clustered into the Quadrilatero d'Oro (p68) make for a giddy, glamorous jaunt for any fashion-addict worth their slate-grey Prada cashmere cardigan. Paris, New York and London may have equally influential designers, fashion weeks and excellent shops but can't compete with an industry town that lives and breathes fashion and design and takes retail as seriously as it does biotech or engineering. In line with *la bella figura* – the Italian life philosophy that emphasises the importance of maintaining an immaculate public image, the Milanese themselves see shopping as a social responsibility, not a guilty pleasure.

Beyond the just seen-on-the-runway collections and heart-fluttering price tags of the Quad, the rest of the city is also keen to show you its wares. Designer discount outlets can be found in the middle of the city, the suburbs and in the countryside in Piedmont and Switzerland (p145). Milan's interior and industrial designers have showrooms throughout the city, with a number of them in the streets surrounding Piazza San Babila. Younger labels and a hip new breed of multibrand retailers can be found in Brera, Corso Como, Corso Magenta, Porta Ticenese and Navigli while midrange labels and chains line bustling Via Torino, Corso Vercelli and Corso Buenos Aires. Street markets (p116) can be found in most neighbourhoods too.

Back in the centre, Rinascente offers a fabulous range of diffusion labels for men, women and children, accessories, a sprawling cosmetics floor and a similarly extensive range of homewares. There's also beautiful artisan and regional produce in their rooftop food hall, second only to the legendary Peck (p53).

Shopping hours are generally from 3pm to 7pm Monday, 10am to 7pm Tuesday to Saturday, though many smaller shops still take the traditional lunch break from 12.30pm or 1pm to 3pm or 4pm and some shops, especially in areas such as Navigli and Brera also open on a Sunday. In this book, hours are given in reviews but it's always best to check ahead. Food shops often open on Monday mornings and close in the afternoon.

Right Browse through the addictive array of homewares at Habits Culti (p68)

STYLIST'S EYE
> 10 Corso Como (p103)
> Antonioli (p130)
> Biffi (p131)
> Iris (p69)
> Antonia Boutique (p81)

BEST MENSWEAR
> E.Marinella (p144)
> Host (p146)
> Tom Ford (p69)
> Alberto Aspesi (p65)
> Nana's Thrift Store (p132)

ONLY IN MILAN
> asap (p105)
> Mauro Bolognesi (p132)
> Cavalli e Nastri (p81)
> G. Lorenzi (p67)
> La Vetrina di Beryl (p82)

DESIGNER OUTLETS
> 10 Corso Como Outlet (p103)
> Il Salvagente (p115)
> DMagazine (p67)
> Etro Outlet (p123)
> Mercato Via Fauche (p116)

APERITIVO

Forget all your preconceptions of happy hour. First off, stretch that hour into three (generally from 6pm to 9pm, though the Milanese rarely get there before 7pm). Secondly, expect your cocktail to be expertly mixed and strong, not luridly coloured and wearing fruit. Thirdly, while there may well be crisps and roast nuts on offer, they'll be joined by a tasty, complimentary, and often surprisingly healthy buffet, and finally, almost no one gets bladdered, lagered, shit-faced or otherwise messy; the Milanese are quite happy to stop at one Negroni and often do.

Drink prices range from €4 to €8, but be prepared to fork out up to €15 at some of the more luxe hotels. Usually the higher the drink price, the more lavish the buffet, though sometimes you're paying for a bar's fashion cred rather than wild salmon *crudo* (raw). Though at €8-plus places you are likely see a lot of raw fish, oysters, prosciutto, salami and roast beef, barley and trout salads, chickpeas and couscous, cauliflower and cardoon fritters, baked ricotta, *caprese* (mozarella, tomato and basil) salad on a stick, and a few platters of hot pasta. Simpler spreads make the most of pizza, crostini and bruschetta, with cured meats, cheese, grilled eggplant and smoked salmon being the favoured topping and *frittata, arrancini,* potato croquettes, gratined peppers and olives often making an appearance too.

Most, but not all, bars offer *aperitivi*; call to check or wander by and look for the crowds. There are a few areas that will yield lots of choice in a small radius: Corso Sempione and Corso Como for a bit of glam or Corso Buenos Aires and Navigli for a more laid-back vibe. *Milano2night* (http://milano.tonight.eu) has extensive listings of new bars, as does the print edition of *Vivimilano* (www.vivimilano.it) in Wednesday's *Corriere della Sera*. Travellers can also check out **Aperonet** (http://aperonet.jimdo.com) for a weekly roster of *aperitivo* meet-ups.

BIG NIGHT OUT APERITIVO	LOW-KEY APERITIVO
> Living (p98)	> Le Biciclette (p137)
> Milano (p98)	> Bar Basso (p73)
> Diana Garden (p73; pictured right)	> Café Portnoy (p137)
> Noon (p149)	> Obika (p85)
> Il Marchesino (p52)	> Frida (p108)

FOOD

The food of Milan may not be redolent of the sun, like that of the south, but its quintessential dishes are still richly golden-hued. *Cotoletta*, sliced buttery veal with a burnished breadcrumb crust recalling the Austrian Empire, and mellow yellow risotto Milanese, Po Valley *carnaroli* rice enriched with bone marrow and tinted with saffron, are cases in point. Other gold standards include *osso bucco*, a veal shank stew scattered with spritzy *gremolata* (parsley, garlic and lemon-rind); spring-bright zucchini flowers; the polenta that accompanies meat or mushroom dishes; pumpkin-stuffed sage-scented ravioli; *panettone*, the eggy, brioche-like Christmas bread; *mostarda di frutta*, Cremona's ancient mustard-laced sweet preserves, and Lombard's rich bounty of cheese (p114).

Genovese and Piedmontese dishes often share menu space with the local lads; *trofie* (pasta twists) with pesto, potatoes and green beans and onion-strewn focaccia here, *bollito misto* (mixed boiled meats) and *fonduta* (fondue) there. As well as the food of these near neighbours, Milan's generations of immigrants from throughout Italy mean that dishes from most regions pop up regularly and restaurants serving the staples of Lazio, Campagnia, Tuscany and Puglia are easy to find. The city's increasingly diverse global population is also reflected in the city's eating habits. Unusually for Italy, Japanese and Chinese restaurants are commonplace (see p84 for a look at sushi *alla Milanese*) and the cuisines of India, Latin America, the Middle East and both North and sub-Saharan Africa are all represented.

The Milanese love keeping up with their own restaurant scene, which includes a clutch of Michelin-starred chefs who cook some of Italy's most innovative and sophisticated food. Some deconstruct regional standards, others imbue them with new-world twists; while the culinary antics are hotly debated, produce is always sublime and the results often stunning. In lesser hands, though, the experimental verve can be downright silly and the PR hype as tired as the fusion on the plate.

Restaurant guides to look for are Corriere della Sera's *Vivimilano* (www.vivimilano.it), *Gambero Rosso* (www.gamberorosso.it), the free Zero Milano's annual guide (milano.zero.eu) and *Pappamondo*, a guide to more than 450 ethnic restaurants and food shops; all in Italian but simple to follow.

Right Get your fix of raw fish at Pescheria da Claudio (p86)

BEST MOD ITALIAN
> Cracco (p55)
> Sadler (p137)
> Trussardi alla Scala Ristorante (p55)
> Don Carlos (p70)
> D'o (p147)

CLASSIC COTOLETTA
> Antica Trattoria della Pesa (p106)
> Il Marchesino (p52)
> Il Baretto al Baglioni (p71)
> Trattoria di Giannino (p73)
> Maiao (p52)

PERFECT PASTICCERIAS
> Sissi (p118)
> Princi (p54)
> Pasticceria Cucchi (p148)
> Marchesi (p53)
> Giovanni Galli (p56)

BEST GELATI
> GROM (p51)
> Chocolat (p147)
> Riva Reno (p136)
> Gelateria Marghera (p147)
> Gelateria Le Colonne (p135)

DESIGN

From the cup that holds your morning espresso to the bedside light you click off before bed, there's a designer responsible, and almost everyone in Milan will know their name. Design here is a way of life.

Italian design's roots are in 1930s Milan, with the opening of the Triennale, the founding of *Domus* and *Casabella* magazines, Rinascente's visionary commissions and the development of the Fiera. Milan today is home to all the major design showrooms and the site of an endless round of influential international design fairs, and continues to be a centre of design education and publishing.

While the modernist ideal of creating useful objects is at Italian design's core, it's not so easy to define its style. Design in Italy is suffused with emotion and desire, it's expressive and individual. Large-scale industrial production came late; this meant that a decorative joy persisted in spite of modernist rigour. And the cultural memory of Latin animism – ancient Roman household objects had a spirit – is present too. Lounge on Zanuso's Lady chair, tear around on a Piaggio Ciao, toss something into Enzo Mari's *in attesa* waste-paper basket; they breathe.

A visit to the Design Museum at the Triennale is a wonderful way to pay homage to the work of Italy's best and brightest. Many of these called, or continue to call, Milan home; the names to watch for include Gio Ponti, Bruno Munari, Piero Fornasetti, Enzo Mari, the Castiglioni brothers, Gaetano Pesce, Mario Bellini, Gae Aulenti, Ettore Sottsass and Alessandro Mendini.

DESIGN INSPIRATION
> Triennale di Milano (p94)
> Studio Museo Achille Castiglioni (p92)
> Design Library (p130)
> 10 Corso Como bookshop (p103)
> Wannenes il XX Secolo (p69)

CHICEST SHOWROOMS & SPAZIO
> É de Padova (p114; pictured top left)
> Spazio Rossana Orlandi (p146; pictured above)
> Danese (p122)
> Cassina (p113)
> B&B Italia (p113)

SNAPSHOTS

MUSEUMS & GALLERIES

Milan's bijou museums contain priceless collections from the early-Renaissance to the neoclassical. You can often linger with a Bellini, Michelangelo, Mantegna, Caravaggio, Tintoretto or Canova without the usual throng of crowds, even in Milan's most famous gallery, the Brera Pinacoteca.

The city is also a treasure trove of 20th-century Italian work. At the Galleria d'Arte Moderna (the Divisionists, Italy's rather sentimental answer to impressionism, violently morph into Futurism in front of your eyes. The work of Umberto Boccioni and Giacomo Balla is, a hundred years on, shockingly fresh and eerily prescient of the tumultuous times the next decades would bring.

The walls of Villa Necchi-Campiglio are hung with a far more gentle but nonetheless beguiling collection of paintings by Giorgio Morandi and Massimo Campigli. The Casa Museo Boschi-di Stefano boasts paintings from Giorgio di Chirico and the Paris school of Italian surrealists, the work of the abstract-expressionist Informels, as well as the slashed and bubbling canvases from the ever-experimental Lucio Fontana and early conceptualist Piero Manzoni.

As for this century, Milan's artworld resignedly awaits a museum of contemporary art, slated as part of the CityLife project. In the meantime, the scene is buoyed by canny commercial galleries, risk-taking private foundations and the small-scale civic museums like Palazzo Reale (p43) and Padiglione d'Arte Contemporanea (PAC; p64). There are few nonprofit or artist-run spaces but organisations such as Careof, Docva & Viafarini (p89) and Assab One (www.assab-one.org) tap into the energy of the city's emerging generation of artists.

BEST COLLECTIONS

> Pinacoteca di Brera (p77)
> Pinacoteca Ambrosiana (p46)
> Palazzo Reale (p43)
> Galleria d'Arte Moderna (p62)
> Casa Museo di Boschi-di Stefano (p62)

SHOCK OF THE NEW

> Massimo de Carlo (p104)
> Galleria Raffaella Cortese (p63)
> Galleria Lia Rumma (p102)
> Fondazione Prada (p122)
> Fondazione Nicola Trussardi (www.fondazionenicolatrussardi.com)

ARCHITECTURE

The allied bombs of WWII wreaked a terrible toll on the city of Milan, and many of the gaping holes were filled in all too quickly. But dotted among the hasty post-war workarounds are fabulously unfussed-over Roman ruins, serene early Christian basilica, hidden Renaissance courtyards and grand 18th-century *palazzo*.

Milan's architectural charm is an excitingly eclectic mix of styles. The city is where Italy's 20th-century design heritage is at the fore. Wide streets are lined with the elegant fin-de-siècle Liberty apartment buildings, and the 1930s Rationalist rigour of Piero Portaluppi merges with the Fascist myth-making of Giuseppe Terragni. And the post-war years *did* yield glorious gems amid the missteps, including two of the world's most unique midcentury skyscrapers – BBPR's Torre Velasca and Gio Ponti's Torre Pirelli – and any number of clever-clever post-modern interiors and inventive industrial refits.

The Milanese often carp that despite claims they are Italy's most modern city, they've not been able to produce a significant new building for over 50 years (Massimiliano Fukas' extraordinary Fiero site in Rho aside). This is about to change: the sound of jackhammers rings through the city as several new urban-redevelopment projects take shape (for a rundown, see p179).

ICONIC 20TH-CENTURY BUILDINGS

> Torre Pirelli (p103)
> Triennale di Milano (p94)
> Torre Velasca (p48)
> Stazione Centrale (p102)
> Torre Branca (p94)

MUST-SEE INTERIORS

> Villa Necchi-Campiglio (p22; pictured right)
> Studio Museo Achille Castiglioni (p92)
> Bulgari Hotel (p86)
> Café Trussardi (p51)
> Viktor & Rolf (p68)

CLUBBING

Milan's frenetic pace doesn't slow after midnight. Going out clubbing here is as cherished a ritual as *aperitivi*, with one often segueing into the other. The scene traverses the spectrum from blithely, blandly commercial to extremely cutting edge, but making an effort applies across the board: glamming up is obligatory and flashing the cash often necessary. Entry runs from €10 to upwards of €20, with some clubs requiring you to 'buy' a table (with a bottle of spirits thrown in with the furniture) for €100 to €200. While club popularity is surprisingly stable – Plastic has been in the business for 24 years – keeping up with nights and DJs is not easy. Zero's fortnightly guide is useful, as is *Milano2night* (www.milanotonight.it).

An alternative to mainstream clubbing is offered by venues under the Italian Recreative and Cultural Association (ARCI) umbrella, an organisation that grew out of the left-wing, anti-Fascist *centri sociali* (social centres) from the 1950s. Today these clubs are part of Milan's nightlife landscape. ARCI *centri sociali* clubs are listed in regular guides; look for Leoncavallo (p109), Casa 139 (p124), Bitte, Biko and Magnolia. You may need to purchase a membership on your first visit (around €13).

Milan's stylish population will scramble even the most fine-tuned gaydar: everyone can work a look and no one plays to type. Most clubs mix a straight, gay and whatever-rocks-your-world clientele. Even at landmark gay/lesbian bars most nights are straight-friendly. Designated 'gay' nights at otherwise 'straight' clubs attract the same unpredictable roll-up.

It's no Oxford St, Soho or West Village, but a small dedicated club strip is located in Via Sammartini, on the western side of Stazione Centrale, and this is where you'll find the majority of cruising venues. **Centro d'Iniziativa Gay-ArciGay Milano** (☎ 02 541 22 225; www.arcigaymilano.org, in Italian; Via Bezzeca 3) provides information for gay and lesbian visitors, and can arrange the ARCI passes that are required to get into some places.

BEST CLUBS

> Plastic (p126)
> Magazzini Generali (p126)
> Rocket (p138)
> Gasoline Club (p109)
> Gattopardo (p99)

BEST GAY NIGHTS

> Nuova Idea (p109)
> Plastic (p126)
> G-Lounge (p56)
> Barbarella's Glitter (www.myspace
  .com/yearsofglitter)

MUSIC

The city of Verdi and Puccini has been home to some of the world's foremost classical musicians for at least two centuries as well as the toughest audiences. The electric air of expectation fills Milan's concert halls with collective adrenaline, pushing musicians to perform even when the house is half-empty. Concerts begin with audiences already on the edge of their seats, knowing that the musicians risk immediate, vocal derision if they fail to reach new heights; but when they succeed, the euphoria of the crowd is like none other.

La Scala and the Auditorium di Milano's Giuseppe Verdi Orchestra aren't the only shows in town. Home to more than 20 independent labels and Italy's major music publishers, Milan is also famous for jazz and an alternative scene featuring earnest but affecting singer-songwriters and fun, suspiciously well-groomed power-pop and punk bands. Like any city in Italy, you'll have to tune out to the school of San Remo pop ballads, repetitive generic dance and cringe-worthy hip hop. But the Milanese are in the indie loop and firmly on the tour circuit of the best British, Swedish, French and North American acts. Watch out for gigs at Rolling Stone, Magazzini Generali, Plastic and wicked summer festival line-ups.

Catch a performance at Milan's revered opera house, Teatro la Scala (p48)

FIERA

Milan's two fairgrounds (*fiera*) play host to an endless round of trade fairs and conventions, from microelectronics meet-ups to the biannual block-busters Moda Donna and Moda Uomo, better known as Milan fashion weeks. Massimiliano Fuksas' brilliantly engineered Fiera Milano exhibition space was built on the Agip oil refinery in Rho-Pero, around 40 minutes out of town by metro. In action since 2006, its billowing glass-and-steel sail (the complex's Italian nickname '*la vela*' means just that) floats over 1.4km of various halls and supporting areas, capable of holding up to half a million visitors. The city's historic fairgrounds just northwest of Parco Sempione are the site of the CityLife redevelopment but smaller fairs are still held at the remaining pavilions, known as Fiera Milano City.

As well as Milan's famous fashion weeks, the most high profile of the fairs is the Salone Internazionale del Mobile held annually in April. It attracts around 300,000 visitors and creates city-wide mayhem. The Salone del Mobile also takes over Zona Tortona, to the south of Porta Genova; satellite events are held at venues including the legendary Superstudio Più.

The Rho-Pera move means proximity to the red (M1) metro line is really all that matters for travellers when booking accommodation. If you're coming to town for a large fair or convention, be sure to book ahead for anything that's not already spoken for in your itinerary, be that accommodation, restaurants, spa treatments, airport pick-ups or tickets to La Scala.

Milan is renowned the world over for its dazzling array of fashion shows at Milan Fashion Weeks (p28)

Art in Milan has always been about innovation

BACKGROUND

HISTORY

PLAIN OLD MILAN

Several millennia ago, Lombardy's first designers set to zealously decorating their surrounds; the rocky Val Camonica to Milan's northeast is covered in engraved petroglyphs gleefully depicting figures hunting, farming, making magic and indulging in wild sexual antics. According to legend, the Insubri Celts chose the site of Milan around 400 BC, when their greedy king glimpsed a bristle-backed boar across the plains.

The Roman's didn't consider wild Cisalpine Gaul part of Italy at all, though they liked what they saw. In 222 BC, after a few centuries of skirmish, they conquered the city they went on to name Mediolanum (middle of the plains). The Insubres didn't exactly roll over, and during Hannibal's invasion a few years later sided with the Carthaginians. Despite the superior design of their chariots and poleaxes, they were on the wrong side of history. By 49 BC, they too were proudly mouthing *civis Romanus sum* (I am a Roman citizen).

Mediolanum suppled arms for the Empire's insatiable war machine and prospered on the Roman road to the northwest. The Lakes became a favoured holiday destination for the Roman elite; it was to a villa in Sirmione that the poet Catullus retreated when 1st-century-BC it-girl Clodia Metelli broke his heart. As the Empire crumbled in the 4th century, Mediolanum, with its strategic position by the Rhine frontier, became home to the imperial court. Roman ruins from this time are scattered throughout the city – including the columns of San Lorenzo and the palace ruins in the Via Brisa. It was from Mediolanum that Emperor Constantine made his momentous edict granting Christians freedom of worship in AD 313.

HUNS, GOTHS, LOMBARDS & A HOLY TERROR

Attila the Hun and various Goths had their way with the city before the Germanic Lombards took over in 569. Beloved Lombard Queen Theodolinda managed to bring the locals in line with the mainstream Roman church. But the Franks were at the door – Charlemagne claimed Milan for the Holy Roman Empire in 774.

By the 11th century Milan had formed an ambitious canal-building commune, and was then besieged and all but destroyed by the Holy Roman Emperor Frederick Barbarossa. He was in turn defeated by the newly formed Lega Lombarda in 1176.

DEATH & DYNASTIES

Medieval Milan flourished on the back of textile and arms manufacturing as well as its fertile and well-managed farmlands to the south (an industry mix not too dissimilar to today) and the Visconti dynasty attracted Italy's best artisans. Work began on the Duomo in 1386, the marble transported to Milan via newly built canals. Unfortunately, plague-infested rats came along for the ride. More than 30,000 Milanese died.

Ludovico Sforza took control in the 1480s. His brilliant wife Beatrice d'Este is widely credited with luring da Vinci and Bramante to Milan. The French usurped the Sforzas in 1499, but with more epidemics between 1524 and 1528 the weakened city fell under Spanish rule in 1535. Plague-ridden Milan offered more trouble than tax revenue to the Spaniards, and was handed to the Austrians in 1713. The city blossomed again under stylish Empress Maria Theresa, and the facades of La Scala and the Palazzo Reale remain her favourite shade of parchment yellow.

NEW ITALY

Napoleon chose Milan as the capital of his new-fashioned Cisalpine Empire in 1795. He retook the city in 1805, immediately crowning himself king of Italy. His time was short, but he had a huge impact on the city both architecturally and psychologically.

Austrian rule returned with Napoleon's demise in 1814, but the seeds of Italian unification had been sown. The Cinque Giornate, the five days of Milan, was the city's bloody to-the-barricades moment of 1848. Austrian commander Josef Radetzky recaptured the city but troops commandeered by Vittorio Emanuele II and Napoleon III finally defeated the Austrians at the Battle of Magenta in 1859. Milan celebrated joining the nascent Kingdom of Italy in 1860 with a binge on opulent architecture, from the morbidly glamorous Cimitero Monumentale to the glitzy Galleria Vittorio Emanuele II.

Unification proved good for business. While Italy had all but missed the first Industrial Revolution, Milan was uniquely positioned to take advantage of second-wave technologies like the combustion engine and electricity. But not everyone was enjoying good times. Workers staged some of Europe's first mass strikes in 1872. Italy's first socialist party was founded in Milan 10 years later as recession hit, and in May 1898 over a hundred people were killed when four days of demonstrations were crushed with cannons and gunfire.

The new century brought affluence and optimism, but also the frivolous Italietta (Little Italy): a sentimental, consumerist petit-bourgeoisie, of Liberty-style drawing rooms and Puccini opera. Decorative, as the Futurists predicted, was soon to become a dirty word.

BOMBS & BLACKSHIRTS

Milan hadn't yet recovered from its WWI losses when influenza struck in 1918, and the economy faltered. Benito Mussolini's political career began in Milan, swiftly moving from words to direct action at the hands of his paramilitary Blackshirts. His promises of strength and national unity had broad appeal and by 1922 he was prime minister (many turned a blind eye to his rapid assumption of absolute power until 1938, when at Hilter's behest, he introduced anti-Semitic 'race laws'). San Siro stadium was built in 1926, embodying Fascism's disconcerting mix of Rationalist modernity and Mussolini's fetish for the camper side of Imperial Rome. The city's other former Fascist monuments include Stazione Centrale, the Triennale, Palazzo dell Arengario and the massive Armani shop on Via Manzotti.

During WWII, the Allied forces destroyed over a quarter of the city, leaving La Scala and the Palazzo Reale in ruins. The Italian Resistance and anti-Fascist trade unions paralysed Milan with strikes and demonstrations in 1943. Italy surrendered to Allied forces on 8 September, but two weeks later Mussolini declared a new Fascist republic in Salò, forcing a long, bloody fight against the Allies and a civil guerrilla war. The partisans prevailed in 1945 and Mussolini was captured near Como as he tried to escape to the border. He was executed along with his mistress, their bodies brought to Milan and displayed at a petrol station. Journalist Rossana Rossanda recalled 'I saw the bodies, Mussolini, Clara Petacci and the others, strung up by their feet in Piazzale Loreto. In front of them there thronged a furious mass of people, women shouting, men white-faced with indignation, screaming out their anger and their impotence: justice had been done by somebody else, on their behalf. There was some derision, but mostly rage. I turned away; it was a necessary ritual, perhaps, but terrible.'

The Cimitero Monumentale (p92) contains a memorial to the Milanese who died in Nazi concentration camps. Designed by Studio BBPR, the pure form of a cube is traced in steel and slab marble, a response of reason and light to the horror of the war years. At its centre is earth from the camp where Gianluigi Banfi, one of BBPR's four partners, died.

COMEBACKS & KICKBACKS

A post-war manufacturing boom produced yet another growth spurt and change was in the air. In 1963 Umberto Eco, chafing against the conformity and insularity of Italian intellectual life, co-founded the avant-garde literary group Gruppo 63. The year 1968 brought dissent, free love and psychedelic fashions to the city's students. The Quadrilatero d'Oro became synonymous with the fashion industry; fashion weeks relocated from Florence in 1971. At the same time, growing income gaps and mass migration from southern Italy inflamed underlying tensions and old political rivalries. Brigade Rosse terrorism and repressive anti-terror laws created further turmoil, giving rise to extremist groups like the Lega Nord (Northern League).

The glamorous '80s and '90s brought stability to Milan, or so it seemed. Corruption and organised crime mushroomed behind closed doors until the Tangentopoli (Bribesville) scandals broke in 1992. Mafia hits and bombs also rocked the city, with a Lega Nord candidate taking the mayorship soon after.

Milan's own Silvio Berlusconi was elected Italian prime minister in 2001, despite owning a huge chunk of the country's media (he also happens to be the nation's third richest man). With a stalling economy and mounting legal and personal drama he was ousted in 2006. Italy confounded the world in 2008 by yet another *crisi*, a parliamentary vote of no confidence, and by going on to again elect Berlusconi. The city's mayoral race in 2006 was close, obliging Berlusconi-anointed centre-right Letizia Moratti (the first female mayor), to form a coalition government with the left.

Milan remains Italy's financial heart and the centre of publishing, media, advertising, design and fashion. With the winning of Expo2015, all eyes are on the horizon.

ART

A young Michelangelo Merisi, now better known by the name of his Lombard home town Caravaggio, got noticed in Milan with his singular style of extreme realism in 1584 while art maverick and true Renaissance man Leonardo da Vinci hung around long enough to paint the *Last Supper* and install a system of locks and levees for the city's canals. Art in Milan has always been about innovation.

Divisionism hit the city in the 1890s, influenced by French neo-impressionist theories. Paintings were built up from small strokes of pure colour. Despite the painting's luminosity, Divisionism's formal constraints and cloying sentimentality often obscure many artist's radical themes.

Futurist painter Gino Severini described the artistic atmosphere of early 20th-century Milan as 'messier and more destructive than you could imagine'. Divisionism's dissection of colour coupled with the alienation and disillusionment of post-Risorgimento Italy gave birth to Futurism. Milan's most famous, and often infamous, art movement was launched upon the world by a gang of drawing-room revolutionaries headed up by the painter, FT Marinetti. His 1910 manifesto railed against museums, the past and even pasta, and looked presciently to a new century forged by violence, war, machines and speed. The movement was a broad church, ranging from Marinetti's card-carrying Fascism to those more interested in aesthetic liberation and the search for a poetic of the industrial age. These included Giacomo Balla, Umberto Boccioni and a young Bruno Munari.

Post WWII, the Informels captured the frustrated but heady energy of the early boom years in paintings marked by 'formlessness'. Initially an Informel, Lucio Fontana went on to poke holes and slash canvases, and with Piero Manzoni, famous for exhibiting cans of 'Artist's Shit', were Italy's seminal conceptual artists. Another, Mario Merz, would go on to become a leading figure in the Arte Povera movement, still highly influential today. Milan continues to be an art-world hub, somewhat troubled but never dull. See Contemporary Art (p24) for more details.

WALL TO WALL

Graffiti has been a consistent in Milan's urban landscape through eras of occupation or repressive rule. As always, politics competes for wall space with declarations of undying love (for a sweetheart or a football team) and gleeful obscenity (often in connection with Megan Gale). Slogans are fast being replaced by elaborate illustrations, 'bombing', tagging and stencilling; images now appear to speak louder than words. Both Via Bramante's northern end and the famous 'Graffiti Bridge' over the metro tracks to Via Tortona are densely decorated. Sundays are good for graffiti spotting; with shop shutters down, paint suddenly reappears.

HIGHER & HIGHER

Always unpredictable, Milan's urban landscape has more surprises in store. The innovative industrial refits for Milan's fashion luminaries continue in Zona Tortona; Garibaldi Porta Nuova is being redeveloped by César Pelli along with the Citta della Moda complex; Renzo Piano is doing up the old Campari factory on the road to Monza and Rem Koolhaas is designing a sprawling multipurpose exhibition space for the Fondazione Prada.

The most significant project of them all is CityLife. International archi-stars Zaha Hadid, Arata Isozaki, Pier Paolo Maggiora and Daniel Libeskind are reinventing the huge old Fiera site, with three individual office towers, housing, parks and a long-awaited museum of contemporary art. Not without controversy though; local residents were outraged at the lack of consultation, and at time of writing, Silvio Berlesconi was objecting to the expressively sculptural towers, with Libeskind then accusing the PM of hating foreigners and preferring Fascism's straight lines. Scheduled completions range from 2010 to Expo's unmovable 2015 deadline. We can't wait for the dust to clear.

GOVERNMENT & POLITICS

Milan has a reputation for extremes – as the birthplace of both Italy's anarchist movement and the ultraconservative, anti-immigration Lega Nord, and home to right-wing PM Silvio Berlusconi and Dario Fo, the Nobel Prize–winning playwright whose own mayoral bid rallied Milan's left. The city's current mayor Letizia Moratti was Berlusconi's preferred candidate but needed to court the left to form a coalition government.

Most Milanese are as vocal about local politics as they are about football – though for many, both are spectator sports. Immigration continues to be a polarising issue and one that rarely produces informed or compassionate debate at any level. Air quality is another. A malevolent haze often hovers over the city, the result of lax industry regulation and emissions from a far too beloved fleet of cars and *motos* (motor scooters). The current trial of a congestion charge, the Ecopass (p54), has yet to show tangible results. Making the metro and the bicycle sexy again might be the city's only hope for clean air.

FURTHER READING

The Futurist Cookbook (FT Marinetti) Recipes that don't look so kooky in these days of molecular gastronomy.

Maurizio Cattelan (Francesco Bonami, Massimiliano Gioni et al) Milan's bad boy artist and king of mockery, pocket-sized.

Design as Art (Bruno Munari) The illuminating gaze of the designer who Picasso called 'the new Leonardo'.

Design City Milan (Cecilia Bolognesi) Photographic tour of cutting-edge architecture and interiors.

Gio Ponti (Ugo La Pietra) Monograph from local publisher Rizzoli.

Gomorrah (Roberto Saviano) Investigative best-seller that has Milan's fashion houses in bed with the Camorra.

The House of Gucci (Sara G Forden) Stranger-than-fiction account of luxury luggage, the Mafia and murder.

Milan Since the Miracle (John Foot) Traces Milan's transformation from manufacturing giant to post-industrial media-mad metropolis.

Accidental Death of an Anarchist (Dario Fo) Sly, subversive comedy by the winner of the 1997 Nobel Prize for Literature and the city's unofficial court jester.

Foucault's Pendulum (Umberto Eco) The semiotician's elaborate Templar-Rosicrucian-Freemason-Jesuit conspiracy unravels in Milan.

Promessi Sposi (The Betrothed; Alessandro Manzoni) The birth of the modern novel in a tale of two lovers, and a country, longing to be united.

MILAN ON FILM

Miracolo a Milano (Miracle in Milan; 1951) This earnest fairy tale from Vittorio de Sica features a boy found in a cabbage patch who unites the poor and is given the gift of miracles.

Rocco and His Brothers (1960) An interesting counterpoint to Fellini's Roman odyssey *La Dolce Vita*, released the same year; Luchino Visconti's controversial film about southern immigration, boxing, brotherhood and urban desolation.

La Notte (The Night; 1961) Michelangelo Antonioni brilliantly evokes Milan's hermetic city streets during a meandering day in the life of a bored and narcissistic couple, played by Marcello Mastroianni and Jeanne Moreau.

Teorema (1968) Pier Paolo Pasolini sets blue-eyed stranger Terence Stamp loose on a haute-bourgeois Milanese family, in a tale of repression, sexual awakening and transcendent yearning.

Tutto a Posto e Niente in Ordine (All Screwed Up; 1973) Better translated as *Everything's in Order But Nothing Works*, Lina Wertmüller's noisy, angry, relentlessly paced comedy crashes its way through Jesus, Marx, Freud and the cult of consumer durables while poignantly portraying the lives of a group of young Southerners.

Salò (1975) Set in the Lombard town of the title that became Mussolini's base after the fall of Milan, Pasolini uses abrupt film work and de Sade's *The 120 Days of Sodom* to construct a truly shocking film about power, pornographic violence, complicity and victimhood.

DIRECTORY
TRANSPORT
ARRIVAL & DEPARTURE
AIR

Most international and some intra-European flights use **Malpensa airport** (www.sea-aeroportimilano .it/en/malpensa/), 50km northwest of the city. The majority of domestic and an increasing number of intra-European flights use **Linate airport** (www.sea-aeroportimilano.it/en/linate/), a far more convenient trip, 7km east of the city centre. For Malpensa and Linate flight information, phone ☎ 02 748 52 200. Budget airlines also use **Orio al Serio airport** (☎ 035 326 323; www.sacbo.it), near Bergamo.

Milan Malpensa

Despite the design input of late, great Ettore Sottsass, Malpensa is one of Europe's worst airports. It's plagued by delays, has an appalling lack of meaningful signage, inadequate services and half-hearted transport links. Don't get us started on the dated po-mo colour scheme.

Milan Linate

Autostradale (☎ 02 339 10 794; www .autostradale.it) buses service Linate airport (one way €4, 25 minutes, every 20 minutes between 5.40am and 9.35pm from Piazza Luigi di Savoia outside Stazione Centrale, and between 6.10am and 11.30pm from Linate). The local ATM bus No 73 (one way €1, 20 minutes, about every 15 minutes between 5.30am and 8pm) runs between the airport and Piazza San Babila (on the corner of Corso Europa).

Orio al Serio Airport

Orioshuttle runs buses around half- hourly from 4.15am to 11.15pm from Piazza Luigi di Savoia outside Stazione Centrale, and from Orio al Serio airport from 4.50am to 12.15am (€6.90/3.45, one hour). There are also regular buses to the airport from Bergamo train station.

Train

The **Malpensa Express** (☎ 02 20 222; www.malpensaexpress.it; ☑ ticket office 7am-8pm) train links Cadorna Stazione Nord with Malpensa (one way €11/5.50, 40 minutes, every 30 minutes). Trains depart from Malpensa Terminal 1 from 6.53am to 9.23pm and from Cadorna between 5.57am and 8.57pm. Outside these hours there are buses at 4.20am and 5am from Cadorna and limited buses to 1.30am from the airport; check the website for timetables. Passengers arriving or departing from Terminal 2 will need to catch a shuttle bus to the Terminal 1 train station or bus pickup point.

DIRECTORY

Bus

Two companies operate coaches to and from both Malpensa terminals to Piazza Luigi di Savoia, outside Stazione Centrale.

Malpensa Shuttle (☎ 02 585 83 185; www.malpensa-shuttle.com; ✆ ticket office 7am-9pm) runs every 20 minutes between 5am and 10.30pm, and approximately hourly throughout the rest of the night (€7/3.50, 50 minutes).

Autostradale leave Malpensa from 6am to 12.30am and Milan from 4.35am to 11pm around every 20 to 30 minutes (€7.50/3.50, 50 minutes).

Taxi

There is a flat fee of €70 to and from Malpensa and central Milan. The drive to Milan should take around 50 minutes outside peak hours.

FLIGHTLESS MILAN

Milan can be reached from London in around 13 hours by daytime TGV. The more leisurely option is to catch a mid-afternoon Eurostar to Paris in time to take the overnight *Stendhal* to Milan, a sleeper and couchette only train. Sleeper fares include morning coffee and croissants as well as access to lounges at each end. Not only do you avoid the hell of Heathrow and the mess of Malpensa, there's wonderful views of French villages and valleys from the day train (and in summer, on the evening train).

TRAIN

Trains run from Stazione Centrale (Piazza Duca d'Aosta) to all major cities in Italy (Information office ☎ 147 88 80 88; ✆ 7am-9pm). Daily trains run to and from Venice (€24, 3½ hours), Florence (€27, 3½ hours), Genoa (€15.50, 1½ hours), Turin (€20, 1½ hours), Rome (€51, 4½ hours) and Naples (€62, 6½ hours); intercity train fares are quoted. Switzerland-bound Cisalpino trains and the French TGV network also depart from here.

Ferrovie Nord Milano (FNM) trains from **Stazione Nord** (Cadorna, www.fnmgroup.it/orario, in Italian; Piazza Luigi Cadorna) connect Milan with Como (€3.50/1.75, one hour, half-hourly) and other regional destinations. Other north-west regional services leave from Stazione Porta Garibaldi (Piazza Sigmund Freud).

BUS

Domestic and international long-distance buses leave from the **bus station** (☎ 02 63 79 01; Piazza Sigmund Freud) opposite Stazione Porta Garibaldi. **Eurolines** (☎ 02 637 90 299; Piazza Sigmund Freud) has a desk here.

GETTING AROUND

Compact and flat, Milan's major sights are easy to reach by foot. For the sprinkling of must-do shops, bars and restaurants across neighbourhoods, the cheap and efficient metro system is an

CLIMATE CHANGE & TRAVEL

Travel – especially air travel – is a significant contributor to global climate change. At Lonely Planet, we believe that all travellers have a responsibility to limit their personal impact. As a result, we have teamed with Rough Guides and other concerned industry partners to support Climate Care, which allows travellers to offset the greenhouse gases they are responsible for with contributions to energy-saving projects and other climate-friendly initiatives in the developing world. Lonely Planet offsets all staff and author travel.

For more information, turn to the responsible travel pages on www.lonelyplanet.com. For details on offsetting your carbon emissions and a carbon calculator, go to www.climatecare.org.

attractive proposition. Trams, despite the labyrinthine nature of their routes, are also a delightful way to cover ground. **ATM** (☎ 800 80 81 81; www.atm-mi.it) oversees the metro and trams, along with an extensive bus network. Free route maps are available from the **ATM InfoPoint** (⌚ 7.45am-8.15pm Mon-Sat) in the Duomo metro station. Tickets are sold at metro stations, tobacconists and newspaper stands.

In this book, the nearest metro station or tram route is noted after the Ⓜ or 🚋 in each listing.

TRAVEL PASSES

If you use public transport, an un-limited *giornaliero* (daily) ticket for bus, tram and metro trains is good value at €3 (or €5.50 for two days). Books of 10 tickets (five double-journey tickets) are €9.20.

METRO

The metro consists of three main underground lines (red M1, green M2, yellow M3) and the

blue suburban line the Passante Ferroviario, and runs from 6am to midnight. A ticket costs €1 prepurchased or bought at the station and is valid for one ride or up to 75 minutes forward travel on ATM buses and trams. Tickets need to be validated on the way into a station but not on the way out. Milan's metro stations were thoughtfully de-signed but a few generations of careless interventions have seen the wonderfully intuitive colour coding and signage go awry at some stations.

TRAM

Milan's trams range from the beloved orange early 20th-century cars to modern lightrail vehicles, crisscrossing and circling the city. They run similar hours to the metro. Tickets must be prepurchased and validated once on board.

BUS

There are more than 50 city bus routes, though most not as useful as metro or trams. Night buses ply the red and yellow metro routes after midnight and run approximately half-hourly.

TAXI

Taxis are reliable but expensive at around €10 for an average short trip. Head for ranks in the centre and outside major train stations or call ☎ 02 40 40, ☎ 02 69 69 or ☎ 02 85 85. Be aware that meters are on from the receipt of call,not from pick up. Hailing taxis is almost always futile.

RADIOBUS

Part of the ATM, these on-call minibuses pick up from designated stops and drive passengers directly to their door. They are available from 8pm to 2am and must be prebooked. Reservations can be made up to three days in advance or by 6pm on the night on ☎ 02 480 34 803 (call ☎ 02 480 34 800 for late pickups). See the ATM website for more details.

TRANSPORT AROUND MILAN

	Duomo	Quadrilatero D'oro	Brera	Navigli	Corso Como	Corso Sempione
Duomo	n/a	walk 7 minutes	walk 10 minutes	tram 20 minutes	metro 20 minutes	tram 20 minutes
Quadrilatero D'oro	walk 7 minutes	n/a	walk 5 minutes	metro 20 minutes	metro & tram 20 minutes	tram 25 minutes
Brera	walk 10 minutes	walk 5 minutes	n/a	metro 10 minutes	walk 15 minutes	tram 10 minutes
Navigli	tram 20 minutes	metro 20 minutes	metro 15 minutes	n/a	metro 20 minutes	metro, 5 minutes, walk 10 minutes
Corso Como	metro 20 minutes	tram & metro 20 minutes	walk 15 minutes	metro 20 minutes	na/	tram 15 minutes
Corso Sempione	tram 20 minutes	tram 25 minutes	tram 10 minutes	walk, 10 minutes, metro minutes	tram 15 minutes	n/a

PRACTICALITIES
BUSINESS HOURS

Shops in central Milan usually open from 3pm to 7pm Monday and from 10am to 7pm Tuesday to Saturday, but elsewhere are often closed from around 1pm to 3pm. Many also close on Sundays. Banks open from 8.30am to 1.30pm and 3.30pm to 4.30pm Monday to Friday. Cafes/bars open from 7am until late, while restaurants open from noon till 3pm and then from 7pm until midnight. Clubs open from around 10pm until 3am or 4am. Most museums and galleries close on Mondays. Almost all businesses will have very limited hours or be closed in August.

DISCOUNTS

In this book concession prices are indicated as adult/concession/child, or adult/child.

ELECTRICITY

Plugs are standard European two round pins:
Voltage 220V
Frequency 50Hz
Cycle AC

EMERGENCIES

24-hour Pharmacy (☎ 02 669 09 35; Stazione Centrale, upper gallery)
Ambulance (☎ 118)
Carabinieri (☎ 112)
Fire (☎ 115)

Farmacia Carlo Erba (☎ 02 87 86 68; Piazza del Duomo 21; ☼ 9pm-8.30am)
Foreigners' Police Office (☎ 02 622 6568; Via Montebello 26)

HOLIDAYS

New Year's Day 1 January
Epiphany 6 January
Easter Monday March/April
Liberation Day 25 April
Labour Day 1 May
Anniversary of the Republic 2 June
Feast of the Assumption 15 August
All Saints Day 1 November
Festa di Sant'Ambrogio 7 December
Feast of the Immaculate Conception 8 December
Christmas Day 25 December
Festa di San Stefano 26 December

INTERNET

Most midrange to deluxe hotels have internet access, though wireless is by no means the norm and even when offered can be patchy.

Parco Sempione has free wi-fi access, but you need to submit ID, sign up and obtain a password at the Aquarium (p92), Triennale (p94) or Torre Branca (p94) for three hours' use. **Internetpoint Underscore** (☎ 02 720 95 780; Cairoli metro, via Dante; ☼ 10am-9pm) is a cute, well-operated internet cafe just near the entrance to the metro. It also does printing and burns CDs. ID is required in most Italian internet cafes (the government sees all internet users as potential terrorists).

Milan's official tourism websites are confusingly designed and poorly maintained, but are OK for listings of civic museums and the like. Below we've also included other sites useful for keeping up with news, events and recently opened shops, bars, restaurants:

Ciao Milano (www.ciaomilano.it)

Milan City Tourism (www.turismo .comune.milano.it)

Milano da Bere (www.milanodabere.it)

Milano Today (www.apcom.net /milano_today/latestnewsmilan .shtml)

Milano2Night (milano.tonight.eu)

Province of Milan Tourism (www .provincia.milano.it/turismo)

Also see Newspapers & Magazines (opposite).

LANGUAGE
Basics

Hello.	*Buongiorno.* (pol)
	Ciao. (inf)
Goodbye.	*Arrivederci.* (pol)
	Ciao. (inf)
Yes.	*Sì.*
No.	*No.*
Please.	*Per favore*
Thank you.	*Grazie.*
You're welcome.	*Prego.*
Excuse me.	*Scusi.*
I'm sorry.	*Mi dispiace.*

Do you speak English?	
	Parla inglese?
I don't understand.	
	Non capisco.
How much is this?	
	Quanto costa questo?

Getting Around

I'd like a … ticket.	
Vorrei un biglietto di …	
one way	*solo andata*
return	*andata e ritorno*

Where is …?	*Dov'è è …?*
Go straight ahead.	
	Si va sempre diritto.
Turn left/right.	
	Giri a sinistra/destra.

Eating

breakfast	*prima colazione*
lunch	*pranzo*
dinner	*cena*
The bill,	*Il conto,*
please	*per favore*

Shopping

I'm just looking.	
	Sto solo guardando.
What time do you open/close?	
	A che ora si apre/chiudi?
Do you accept credit cards?	
	Accettate carte di credito?
Where's the nearest ATM?	
	Dov'è il bancomat più vicino?

Time, Days & Numbers

What time is it?	
	Che ora è?

today	oggi
tomorrow	domani
yesterday	ieri
morning	mattina
afternoon	pomeriggio
day	giorno

Monday	lunedì
Tuesday	martedì
Wednesday	mercoledì
Thursday	giovedì
Friday	venerdì
Saturday	sabato
Sunday	domenica

1	uno
2	due
3	tre
4	quattro
5	cinque
6	sei
7	sette
8	otto
9	nove
10	dieci
100	cento
1000	mille

MONEY

Milan is Italy's most expensive city and one of the world's top 10. Cheap public transport and all those *aperitivi* buffets aside, it's not a city that lends itself to slumming. Plan to spend at least €120 per person per day, after accommodation costs, and much more if you plan to do some fine dining or can't say no to Prada.

For currency exchange rates, see the Quick Reference inside the front cover.

NEWSPAPERS & MAGAZINES

Milan's most well-known daily newspaper is the staid but moderate *Corriere della Sera* (www .corriere.it). It now also publishes *L'Europeo*, a monthly current affairs and culture monograph known for quality writing and photography (there's English text at the back). Milan's other major daily is *Il Giornale* (www .ilgiornale.it), once owned by Silvio Berlusconi, now published by his brother. Milan's business daily is *Milano Finanza* (www.milan ofinanza.it). Politically independent *La Repubblica* and its weekly news magazine *l'espresso* (espresso.repubblica.it) are published in Rome but its business section comes out of Milan. Two handy general English-language papers are *Hello Milano* (www .hellomilano.it) and *Easy Milano* (www.easymilano.it). The tourist office puts out a free monthly events guide called *MilanoMese*.

The following magazines and guides are mostly available online as well as in print and are good for gleaning a local's perspective on design, fashion, art, food and nightlife:

Casabella
Domus (www.domusweb.it)
Flashart Italy (www.flashartonline.it)
Interni (www.internimagazine.it)
Rodeo (www.rodeomagazine.it/guide /cities/milano)
ViviMilano (www.vivimilano.it/) In *Corriere della Sera*
Urban (www.urbanmagazine.it)
Zero (milano.zero.eu)

TELEPHONE

MOBILES

Prepagato (prepaid) accounts for GSM, dual- or tri-band mobile phones can be purchased from TIM (Telecom Italia Mobile) or Vodafone Italia. Providers also sell SIM cards that gives you an Italian mobile-phone number and *ricarica* (charge cards) can be purchased from most tobacconists. To buy a SIM card, you'll need to supply your passport and the address of your accommodation.

CODES & NUMBERS

International direct dial code	☎ 00
Country code	☎ 39
City code (precedes local numbers)	☎ 02
Local directory inquiries	☎ 12

TIPPING

If service isn't included on the bill, leave a 10% to 15% tip. If it is, leave a little extra for good service.

In bars, small change is fine. Tipping isn't expected by taxi drivers, but staff at luxe hotels are another story.

TOURIST INFORMATION

For maps and brochures, the **main tourist office** (☎ 02 725 24 301; www.prov incia.milano.it/turismo; lower level, Piazza del Duomo 19a; ⏰ 8.45am-1pm, 2-6pm Mon-Sat, 9am-1pm & 2-5pm Sun). There's little in the way of service or advice, though independent operators are quite keen to sell tours. The office maintains listings of hotels but no booking facility. Offices are also located at Linate (☎ 02 702 00 443; ⏰ 9am-5pm Mon-Fri), **Malpensa** (☎ 02 748 67 213; ⏰ 9am-5pm Mon-Fri) and **Stazione Centrale** (☎ 02 725 24 360; ⏰ 8am-7pm Mon-Sat, 9am-noon & 1.30-6pm Sun).

TRAVELLERS WITH DISABILITIES

Milan is not an easy destination for disabled travellers. But for those with limited mobility, ATM has recently introduced low-floor buses on many of its routes and some metro stations are equipped with lifts. See the dual-language **Milano Per Tutti** (www.milanopertutti.it) for details as well as itineraries of accessible sights.

>INDEX

See also separate subindexes for See (p196), Shop (p197), Eat (p198), Drink (p199) and Play (p199).

A

AC Milan 30, 131
accommodation 158-9
air travel 181
aperitivo 162
architecture 169
    Padiglione d'Arte
      Contemporanea 64
    Spazio Oberdan 65
    Stazione Centrale 102
Arco della Pace 98
Armani, Giorgio 68
art 24, 168, 177-8
    festivals 28-9
art galleries 24, 108, *see also*
  See *subindex*
attractions, *see also* See
  subindex
    around Duomo 43-8
    around Parco Sempione
      89-94
    Brera 77-81
    Corso Como, Porta
      Garibaldi & Isola 102-3
    Corso Magenta,
      Sant'Ambrogio & the
      West 142-3
    Navigli, Porta Ticinese &
      Zona Tortona 130
    Porta Romana 122
    Quadrilatero D'Oro 62-5
    San Babila 112-13

B

B&Bs 159
bars, *see* Drink *subindex*

Basilica di Sant'Ambrogio 142
Bellagio 153
Bergamo 152
Berlusconi, Silvio 177
Biblioteca Ambrosiana 46
boat cruises 138
books 179-80
Brera 76-87, **78-9**
bus travel
    to/from Milan 182
    to/from the airports 182
    within Milan 184
business hours 160, 185

C

Capodanno Cinese 28
car travel 54
Careof, Docva & ViaFarini 89
Carnevale Ambrosian 28
Casa Museo Boschi-Di
  Stefano 62
Castello Sforzesco 89, 92
cathedrals, *see individual
  entries*, See *subindex*
cell phones 188
cheese 114
Chiesa di San Francesco 142-3
children, travel with
    aquariums 92
    museums 143
    planetariums 64
Chinatown 96
Christopher Street Day 29
churches & cathedrals, *see individual entries*, See *subindex*
Cimitero Monumentale 92
cinemas, *see* Play *subindex*

Civico Acquario 92
climate change 183
clothes, *see* fashion, Shop
  subindex
clubbing 170, *see also* Play
  subindex
coffee 52
Corso Como area 100-9
Corso Magenta area 140-50,
  141
Corteo dei Re Magi 28
Cortili Aperti 29
costs, *see inside front cover*
Costume National 68
crudo 84

D

dance festivals 30
design 28, 166-8, *see
  also* fashion
Design Library 130
d'Este, Beatrice 175
disabilities, travellers with 188
Dolce & Gabbana 68
drinking, *see also* drinks,
  Drink *subindex*
    around Duomo 56
    around Parco Sempione
      97-9
    Brera 86-7
    Corso Como, Porta
      Garibaldi & Isola 108
    Corso Magenta,
      Sant'Ambrogio & the
      West 149-50
    Navigli, Porta Ticinese &
      Zona Tortona 137-8

drinking continued
    Porta Romana 124
    Quadrilatero D'Oro 73-4
drinks
    aperitivo 162
    coffee 52
    wine 87

E

eating, *see also* food, Eat
    subindex
    around Duomo 50-6
    around Parco Sempione
      95-7
    Brera 84-6
    Corso Magenta,
      Sant'Ambrogio & the
      West 147-9
    Navigli, Porta Ticinese &
      Zona Tortona 134-7
    Porta Romana 123-4
    Quadrilatero D'Oro 70-3
    San Babila 118-19
Ecopass 54
electricity 185
emergencies 185
entertainment, *see also* Play
    subindex
    around Duomo 56-7
    around Parco Sempione
      99
    Brera 87
    Corso Como, Porta
      Garibaldi & Isola 108-9
    Corso Magenta,
      Sant'Ambrogio & the
      West 150
    Navigli, Porta Ticinese &
      Zona Tortona 138-9

Porta Romana 124-7
Quadrilatero D'Oro 74-5
travel to/from major
    stadiums 126
Etro 66
exchange rates, *see inside
front cover*

F

fashion 25, *see also* Shop
    subindex
    designers 68
    labels 66
    Milan Fashion Weeks
      172
    outlets 145
    shows 28
Festa del Naviglio 29
Festa di Sant'Ambrogio 32
festivals
    art 28-9
    Carnevale 28
    crafts 32
    dance 30
    film 30
    flowers 28
    food 32
    gay & lesbian 29
    music 30
    parades 28
Fiera 172
Fiera degli Obei Obei 32
FilaForum 126
Fo, Dario 47
Fondazione Arnaldo
    Pomodoro 130
Fondazione Prada 122
food 164, *see also* eating, Eat
    subindex
    aperitivo 162
    books 179
    cheese 114

crudo 84
festivals 32
football 26, 30, 131

G

Galleria Carla Sozzani 102
Galleria Christian Stein 112
Galleria d'Arte Moderna 62
Galleria Emi Fontana 122
Galleria Francesca Kaufmann
    77
Galleria Gió Marconi 62
Galleria lia Rumma 102
Galleria Raffaella Cortese 63
Galleria Tega 63
Galleria Vittorio Emanuele
    II 43
galleries 24, 168, *see also* See
    subindex
gardens, *see* parks &
    gardens
Garibaldi Porta Nuova 179
gay travellers
    festivals 29
    information 170
Giardini Pubblici 63
Giro d'Italia 29
graffiti 94, 178
grand prix 30
Gucci 66, 68

H

Hangar Bicocca 103
history 174-80
holidays 185
hotels 158

I

Idroscalo Idyll 112
Il Cenacolo 143
Il Duomo 43
Il Duomo area 42-57, **44-5**
Inter Milan 30, 131

000 map pages

International Gay & Lesbian
   Milan Film Festival 29-30
internet access 185-6
Isola 100-9
Italian F1 Grand Prix 30
itineraries 35-7

J
jazz music 171
jogging 63

L
La Bella Estate 30
La Nivola e il Santo Chiodo
   31
La Scala Season Opening 32
Lago Maggiore 155
Lambrate 104
language 186-7
Largo Idroscalo 126
L'Artigiano in Fiera 32
Last Supper, The 143
Latin American Festival 30
lesbian travellers
   festivals 29
   information 170
Livia Simoni Library 48
Lunedì dell'Angelo 28

M
magazines 187-8
markets 116
Marni 68
Mazda Palace 126
Mercatone del Naviglio
   Grande 116
metro 83, 183
MiArt 28
Milan City Marathon 31
Milan Fashion Weeks 172
Milan Linate Airport 181
Milan Malpensa Airport 181
Milano Film Festival 30

Milano Jazzin Festival 30
Milano Musica Festival 30
mobile phones 188
money 187
Monica de Cardenas Galleria
   102
Monlue Festival 30
Moratti, Letizia 177
Museo Bagatti Valsecchi 63
Museo Civico di Storia
   Naturale 63
Museo del Duomo 43
Museo Inter e Milan 131
Museo Nazionale della
   Scienza e della Tecnica 143
Museo Poldi-Pezzoli 63-4
museums 168, see also See
   subindex
music 171, see also Play
   subindex
   festivals 30
Mussolini, Benito 176

N
Navigli 128-39
Naviglio Grande market 116
newspapers 187
nightclubbing 170, see also
   Play subindex

O
opening hours 160, 185
Orio al Serio Airport 181
Orto Botanico 77

P
Padiglione d'Arte
   Contemporanea 64
PalaVobis 126
Palazzo Borromeo 155
Palazzo Madre 155
Palazzo Reale 43, 46
Parco Sempione 92

Parco Sempione area 89-99,
   90-1
parks & gardens
   Giardini Pubblici 63
   Orto Botanico 77
   Parco Sempione 92
Piazza Gramsci 116
Piazza Wagner 116
Piazzale Lagosta 116
Pinacoteca di Brera 77, 81
Planetario Ulrico Hoepli 64
planning 37
politics 179
pollution 54
Porta Garibaldi 100-9, **101**
Porta Romana 120-7, **121**
Porta Ticinese 128-39, **141**
Prada 50, 66, 68
public holidays 185

Q
Quadrilatero D'Oro 58-75,
   60-1

R
racism 96
restaurants, see Eat subindex
Roman Empire 174

S
Salone Internazionale del
   Mobile 29
San Babila 110-19, **111**
San Bernandino alle Ossa 46
San Lorenzo Columns 130
San Lorenzo Maggiore 130
San Siro Stadium 126
Santa Maria Annunciata in
   Chiesa Rossa 122
Santa Maria Presso San Satiro
   46, 48
Sant'Ambrogio area 140-50,
   141

Severini, Gino 178
Sforza, Ludovico 175
shopping 160, see also Shop
    subindex
    around Duomo 48-50
    around Parco Sempione
        94-5
    Brera 81-4
    Corso Como, Porta
        Garibaldi & Isola 103-5
    Corso Magenta,
        Sant'Ambrogio & the
        West 144-7
    markets 116
    Navigli, Porta Ticinese &
        Zona Tortona 130-4
    outlets 145
    Porta Romana 122-3
    Quadrilatero D'Oro 65-70
    sales 28, 30
    San Babila 113-19
soccer, see football
spas, see Play subindex
Spazio Oberdan 65
stained-glass windows 43
Stazione Centrale 102
street art 94
Studio Giangaleazzo Visconti
    112
Studio Guenzani 65
Studio Museo Achille
    Castiglioni 92-4

T
taxi travel 184
Teatro la Scala 48
Teatro la Scala Museum 48
telephone services 188
theatre, see Play subindex

000 map pages

Theresa, Maria 175
tipping 188
Torre Branca 94
Torre Pirelli 103
Torre Rasini 65
Torre Velasca 48
tourist information 188
traffic 54
train travel
    to/from Milan 182
    to/from the airports 181-2
    within Milan 83
travel passes 183
Triennale Bovisa 94
Triennale di Milano 94
Trussardi 66, 68

V
vacations 185
Verona 154
Via Armorari market 116
Via Fauche market 116
Via Fiori Chiari market 116
Via San Marco market 116
Viale Papiniano market 116
views 94
Villa Arconati 126
Villa Arconati Festival 30
Villa Melzi 153
Villa Necchi Campiglio 112-13
Villa Serbelloni 153
Vinilmania 31

W
water sports 112
wine 87
WWI 176
WWII 176

Z
Zona Tortona area 128-39,
    141

👁 SEE

Aquariums
Civico Acquario 92

Castles
Castello Sforzesco 89, 92

Churches & Cathedrals
Basilica di Sant'Ambrogio 142
Chiesa di San Francesco
    142-3
Il Duomo 43
San Babila 112
San Bernardino alle Ossa 46
San Lorenzo Maggiore 130
Santa Maria Annunciata in
    Chiesa Rossa 122
Santa Maria Presso San Satiro
    46, 48

Galleries
Careof, Docva & ViaFarini 89
Casa Museo Boschi-Di
    Stefano 62
Fondazione Prada 122
Galleria Carla Sozzani 102
Galleria Christian Stein 112
Galleria d'Arte Moderna 62
Galleria Emi Fontana 122
Galleria Francesca Kaufmann
    77
Galleria Gió Marconi 62
Galleria Iia Rumma 102
Galleria Raffaella Cortese 63
Galleria Tega 63
Massimo de Carlo 104
Monica de Cardenas Galleria
    102
Pinacoteca Ambrosiana
    46
Pinacoteca di Brera 77, 81
Prometeogallery 104

Studio Giangaleazzo Visconti 112
Triennale Bovisa 94

Libraries
Biblioteca Ambrosiana 46
Design Library 130
Livia Simoni Library 48

Memorials
Cimitero Monumentale 92

Museums
Fondazione Arnaldo Pomodoro 130
Museo Bagatti Valsecchi 63
Museo Civico di Storia Naturale 63
Museo del Duomo 43
Museo Inter e Milan 131
Museo Nazionale della Scienza e della Tecnica 143
Museo Poldi-Pezzoli 63-4
Studio Museo Achille Castiglioni 92-4
Teatro la Scala Museum 48
Triennale di Milano 94

Notable Buildings
Padiglione d'Arte Contemporanea 64
Spazio Oberdan 65
Stazione Centrale 102
Studio Guenzani 65
Villa Necchi Campiglio 112-13

Parks & Gardens
Giardini Pubblici 63
Orto Botanico 77
Parco Sempione 92

Planetariums
Planetario Ulrico Hoepli 64

Ruins
San Lorenzo Columns 130

Towers
Torre Branca 94
Torre Pirelli 103
Torre Rasini 65
Torre Velasca 48

SHOP

Accessories
Fabriano 82
MH Way 117
Nava 117
Piumelli 49-50

Antiques
Al Leone d'Oro 144
Crazy Art 81
Mauro Bolognesi 132
Wannenes il XX Secolo 69-70

Books
10 Corso Como 103
A+M Bookshop 65
Art Book Triennale 94-5
Hoepli International Bookstore 49
Libreria Rizzoli 49

Children's Fashion
Amelia 144
Aprica 65
Frippino 132
I Pinko Palino 69
Nume 146
Pupi Solari 146
Teo 117

Cosmetics
Madina Milano 49

Department Stores
Rinascente 50

Fashion
10 Corso Como Outlet 103
Alberta Ferretti 68
American Apparel 130
Antonia Boutique 81
Antonioli 130-1
asap 105
Aspesi 65-6
Atribu 81
Biffi 131
Bottega del Cashmere 66
Boule de Neige 105
Brazilian 131
Cavalli e Nastri 81
Daad Dantone 67
DMagazine 67
DSquared 68
E. Marinella 144
Elizabeth the First 132
Emilio Pucci 68
Ermenegildo Zegna 68
Etro Profumi 68
Fendi 68
Frip 132
Galleria Rossana Orlandi 145
Gallo 67
Gianfranco Ferré 68
Giorgio Armani 68
Henry Beguelin 145
Il Salvagente 115
i-Milano Tortona 132
Jil Sander 68
Kristina Ti 82
Missoni 66, 68
Miu Miu 68
Moschino 68
Nana's Thrift Store 132, 134

Officina Slowear 95
Paul Smith 69
Prada 50, 66, 68
Roberto Cavalli 68
Showroom ISOLA 105
Suede 146
TAD 83-4
To B 146-7
Tom Ford 69
Trussardi 66, 68
Valentino 68
Versace 66, 68
Viativoli 84
Viktor & Rolf 68

Fashion Outlets
Etro Outlet 123
Fox Town 145
Puma Outlet 123
Serravalle Scrivia 145
The Place 145

Flowers
W Fiori 117

Food & Wine
Eataly 114
L'Altro Vino 115
L'Arte di Offrire il Thé 115
Lula Cioccolato 116
Olivo 117
Venchi 50

Furniture
B&B Italia 113
Cappellini 113
Cassina 113-14
Driade 67
Edra 81-2
Zanotta 117-18

Hats
Borsolino 48-9
Ginger 49

Homewares
Agua del Carmen 144
Danese 122-3
ē De Padova 114
Flos 114
G Lorenzi 67
Guzzini 114
Habits Culti 68
Mr N 82-3
Muji 69
Rigadritto 83
Spazio Rossana Orlandi 146

Jewellery
Anthias 105
Casa di Minea 131
Galante Visconti 82

Music
Buscemi Dischi 144

Perfume
Olfattorio Bar à Parfums 83

Shoes
Car Shoe 66
Iris 69
La Vetrina Di Beryl 82
Zeiss 84

Toys
Citta del Sole 49
Il Mondo é Piccolo 145
Mihai 117

Asian
Bussarakham 134
Jubin 95
La Collina d'Oro 148
Lo's Chinese Takeaway 85
Shri Ganesh 137

Bakeries
California Bakery 118
Princi 106

Cafe Fare
10 Corso Como Café 105
Café Romeo Gigli 134
Caffé della Pusterla 147
Caffé Gucci 50

Crudo
Fingers 123

Enoteca
La Cantina di Via Mussi 96
L'Altra Pharmacia 96

Food Halls
Peck 53-4

French
Piquenique 136

Gelaterie
Chocolat 147
Gelateria le Colonne 135
Gelateria Marghera 147
Grom 51
Riva Reno 136

Health Food
Il GiraSole 148

International
D'o 147

Italian
Acquasala 134
Al Pont de Ferr 134

EAT

African
Dar el Yacout 123
Warsa 73

000 map pages

Antica Trattoria della Pesa 106
Café Trussardi 51
Cantiere dei Sensi 106
Cantina della Vetra 134-5
Chatulle 95
Cracco 55
Da Giacomo 118
Design Library Café 135
Don Carlos 70
El Brellin 135
Emporio Armani Caffè 70-1
Ex Mauri 106
Fioraio Bianchi Caffè 84
Giulio Pane e Ojo 123-4
Gold 118
Il Baretto al Baglioni 71
Il Marchesino 52
Il Salumaio di Montenapoleone 71-2
Il Teatro 72
Joia 72
La Cantina di Manuela 95
Lacerba 124
L'Antico Ristorante Boeucc 52
Latteria 84-5
Le Vigne 136
Maio 52-3
Obika 85
Pane e Acqua 148
Peck Italian Bar 54
Sadler 137
Sergio & Efisio 96-7
Teatro 7 106-8
Trattoria degli Orti 97
Trattoria di Giannino 73
Triennale Design Café 97
Trussardi alla Scala Ristorante 55-6

Japanese
Armani Nobu 70
Iyo 95

Maru 124
Pescheria da Claudio 86
Zero 149

Lebanese
Lyr 96

Mozzarella Bars
Obika 53

Pasticcerie
Caffè Cova 70
Fratelli Freni 51
Marchesi 53
Pasticceria Cucchi 148
Pasticceria Giovanni Galli 56
Princi 54
Sissi 118-19

Pizzerie
Piccola Ishcia 72
Pizzeria del Ticinese 136
Pizzeria Grand'Italia 86
Pizzeria Spontini 72

Seafood
La Cozz 136
L'Oste Scuro 154

Y DRINK

Bars
Art Café 86
Bar Basso 73
Bar Bianco 97
Bar Jamaica 86
Bar Magenta 149
Bhangra Bar 97
Bigne 137
Bulgari Hotel 86
Café PortNoy 137
Capetown Café 137
Chinese Box 108
Diana Garden 73

Frida 108
G-Lounge 56
Just Cavalli Café 73, 98
La Belle Aurore 119
Le Biciclette 137
Le Coquetel 138
l'Elephante Bar 74
Living 98
Martini Bar 74
Milano 98
Noon 149
Nordest Caffè 108
Noy 149
Old Fashion Café 98-9
Posteria de Amici 150
Radetzky Café 108
Roialto 99
Shu 139
Siddharta Buddha Cafe 99
Straf Bar 56
Volo 124
Wagamaga 99

Cafes
Caffè Zucca 56
Lino's Coffee 74

Enoteca
Cantina di Manuela 119
Cantine Isola 97-8
Moscatelli 108
N'Ombra de vin 86-7

Pubs
Birrificio 104
Stalingrado 99

▣ PLAY

Cinemas
Anteospazio Cinema 108
Cinema Mexico 138

INDEX

V

Clubs
Armani Privé 74
Bond 138
Casa 139' 124
Gasoline Club 109
Gattopardo 99
Hollywood 109
La Banque 56-7
Magazzini Generali 126
Nuova Idea 109
Plastic 126
Shocking Club 109
Surfer's Den 126-7

Concerts
Auditorium di Milano 138

Live Music
Blue Note 109
Leoncavallo 109
Rocket 138
Rolling Stone 126
Scimmie 139

Spas
Bulgari Spa 87
Dolce & Gabbana Beauty
  Farm 74

ESPA at Gianfranco Ferré 75
Habits Culti Spa 150
Moresko Hammam 150
Spa Guerlain at Hotel
  Baglioni 75

Theatres
Piccolo Teatro 57
Piccolo Teatro Strehler 87
Teatro Carcano 127
Teatro Grassi 57
Teatro la Scala 48

000 map pages